Design!

FUN
with
Graphics

Peter Owen

Belitha Press

First published in Great Britain in 1993 by
Belitha Press Limited
London House, Great Eastern Wharf,
Parkgate Road, London SW11 4NQ
Text copyright © Celia Rees and Peter Owen
Illustrations copyright © Peter Owen
Format and illustrations copyright © Belitha Press Ltd 1993

Reprinted 1997

Printed in Hong Kong

ISBN 1 85561 204 6 (hardback)
ISBN 1 85561 248 8 (paperback)

British Library Cataloguing in Publication Data CIP
data for this book is available from the British Library

Editor: Jill A. Laidlaw
Designer: Frances McKay
Consultant: Chris Brown

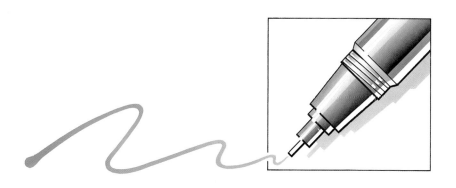

CONTENTS

Words found in **bold** are explained in the glossary
on pages 59-61

Introduction

Graphic design is everywhere. We see it all the time. The cover of this book and the page you are reading are the work of a graphic artist. Anything that conveys a message using words and pictures is graphic design. You only need to look around to see how important and common design is. In advertising, designers create the powerful, clever images that persuade us to go out and buy certain products. In **marketing**, designers provide the bright, attractive packaging that leads us to choose one product rather than another. The cartoons and comics that entertain us and make us laugh, the magazines and newspapers we read, even signs in the street and designs on cars and tee-shirts, are all examples of graphic design.

STARTING OFF
Chapter 1 tells you about the materials and equipment you need to get started.

STARTING TO DESIGN
The *Studio Skills and Techniques* introduced in chapter 2 are based on the work of artists in commercial design studios. The chapter covers a range of essential practical skills including: quick and easy ways to transfer images, different forms of lettering and how to put what you have learnt together in a final paste-up.

THE FIRST DESIGN PROJECT

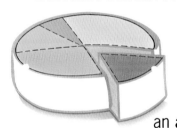

The *Graphic Design* chapter explains how real graphic designers approach and organize their work when taking on an **assignment.** It then takes you, stage by stage,through to the completion of your first design project - to create your own **logo**.

LOOKING GOOD
The *Presentation* chapter explains the importance of good presentation and shows you how to make sure that your work makes an excellent impression.

MAKING CARTOONS AND BOXES
The chapter on *Illustration* explains the basic techniques involved in technical and cartoon drawing. The final chapter on *Paper and Card Engineering* shows you how to design, plan and construct card and paper objects.

THE PROJECTS
The projects in chapters 3 - 6 are fun, easy to follow and are there to help you practise your skills. We hope you will be pleased with what you make and will want to go on to experiment and develop your own ideas for further projects. Whether for yourself or for school, *Design! Fun With Graphics* gives you the know-how and confidence to make all your work clear, effective and eye-catching.

You may wish to go on and learn more or develop your skills further in certain areas, such as drawing cartoons or lettering. Once you have mastered the skills described here, you will be able to find out more about your particular area of interest in any of the excellent specialist books currently on sale. Graphic design is an exciting area in which to work. It influences the man-made world around us. Not all design work is glamorous but whatever the job, designers have to employ a wide range of both practical and creative skills. An understanding of the scope of graphics and the kind of work designers do will help you successfully complete the different projects.

EXPLORING GRAPHICS

Throughout this book, different tips and tricks are explained which offer short-cuts to the best results and are based on the knowledge and know-how of professional artists. The *design projects* offer careful guidance through a series of assignments and there is a comprehensive illustrated glossary on pages 59-61.

DESIGN TIP

When you make a large booklet and need to staple the pages along the centre use your stapler in its open position. Put an eraser under the paper/card to receive the staples, and then bend the staple ends over with your metal ruler.

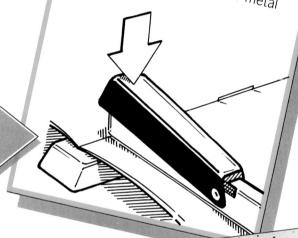

DESIGN PROJECTS

DESIGN PROJECT 1:
A logo for a graphic designer

DESIGN PROJECT 2:
Presentation folder

DESIGN PROJECT 3:
Disco poster

DESIGN PROJECT 4:
Pop-up card

EXAMPLE FROM THE GLOSSARY

burnisher: this looks a little like a screwdriver or a pencil with a flattened metal end. It is used for rubbing dry-transfer lettering through on to paper or card.

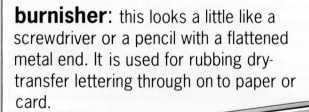

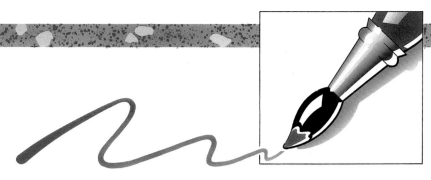

Chapter 1
Materials and Equipment

Graphic designers use a wide range of materials and equipment. This chapter explains the basic items you need for designing. You probably have many of the items described here already. Anything else you require can be bought from good art shops, graphic shops,

DESIGN TIPS
* Keep scraps and off-cuts, they always come in useful.
* Using the right tool for the right job saves time.
* Be extremely careful when handling knives.
* Always cut against a metal cutting edge and on to a cutting mat (see page 9).

office suppliers and stationers. Work out what basic equipment you need to start designing and add other items when you need them. You don't have to buy expensive equipment, a cheap, disposable alternative can do the job just as well, but good equipment can save you money in the long run.

BE ORGANIZED
Once you have the equipment you need, take care of it, keep it organized and use it carefully for the purpose for which it was designed.

Good graphic designers are meticulous; being chaotic wastes time and shows in your work. This means replacing broken items and keeping a check on materials you use regularly so that you do not run out. Do not be wasteful with materials - you can save money if you plan your use of them carefully.

TAKE CARE
Finally, all the items described in this chapter are in regular use in professional design studios. Some pieces of equipment - such as craft knives (see pages 9 and 14) and airbrushes (see pages 8 and 15) - can be dangerous and hazardous if not used properly. These items should always be treated with respect.

WORKING AREA
You need a well lit, comfortable place to work with a **drawing board**, or a slightly raised flat surface.

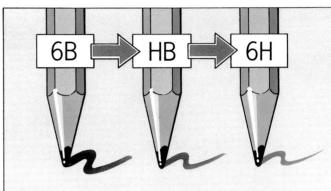

PENCILS
Pencils come in different hardnesses, ranging from 6B which is very soft to 6H which is very hard. The soft B pencils are used for sketching.

HB lead is of normal hardness and you can use it for any pencil work. H to 6H are hard leads and should be used for drawing with instruments and for tracing.

CRAYONS
Thick or thin crayons are available in a wide range of colours. **Water-soluble** crayons can produce **colour washes**.

FELT TIP PENS
Felt tips, with their range of colours and thicknesses, are used for lettering, drawing and roughs.

MARKERS
Markers are useful for covering large areas with colour and for drawing big thick lettering.

TECHNICAL PENS
Technical pens give a consistent thickness of line. They are used for drawing, lettering and illustration.

BRUSHES
A small **sable** brush is useful for lettering and illustration to re-touch or fill in coloured areas. Different thicknesses of brush have different numbers. Brushes are numbered according to their thickness.

AIRBRUSHES
Airbrushes spray ink and air. A basic model, used with an **aerosol propellant**, produces a flat, even colour (see also page 15).

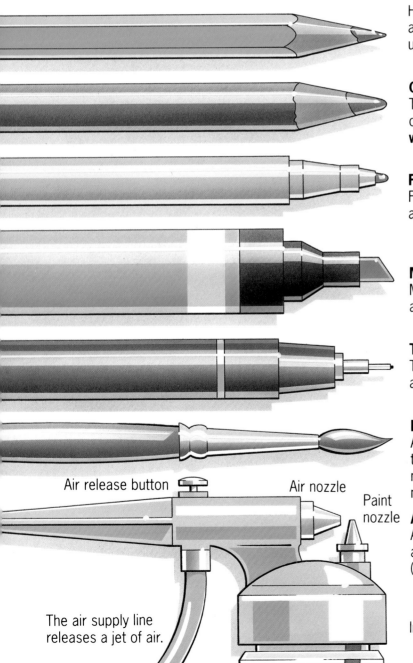

Air release button

Air nozzle

Paint nozzle

The air supply line releases a jet of air.

Ink or paint

SET SQUARES
Set squares come in two different sizes, 60°/30° and 45°.

RULERS
You will need a 60 centimetre plastic ruler, preferably with a **bevelled** edge.

A 30 centimetre metal ruler is also useful.

Metal ruler

Set squares

French curve

FRENCH CURVES
A French curve is a piece of curved plastic. It is useful for drawing curved lines.

TEMPLATES
Templates are a good way of drawing circles and curves accurately.

SCISSORS
Sharp, high quality, scissors are useful.

CRAFT KNIFE
Craft knives cut and scrape marks off board or paper.

COMPASSES
A compass is needed to draw curves and circles.

PROCESS WHITE
A jar of white paint is used for blotting out mistakes.

PROCESS WHITE

ERASERS
A hard eraser is for general use.

A putty eraser removes smudges.

Never use spray glue in an enclosed space. It can be dangerous if inhaled.

PAINT TUBES
A selection of water-based paints in tubes.

GLUE
Spray glue and rubber cement are used for mounting work on to card.

PENCIL SHARPENER
A metal pencil sharpener gives a sharp point to pencils.

INKS
A selection of water-based inks.

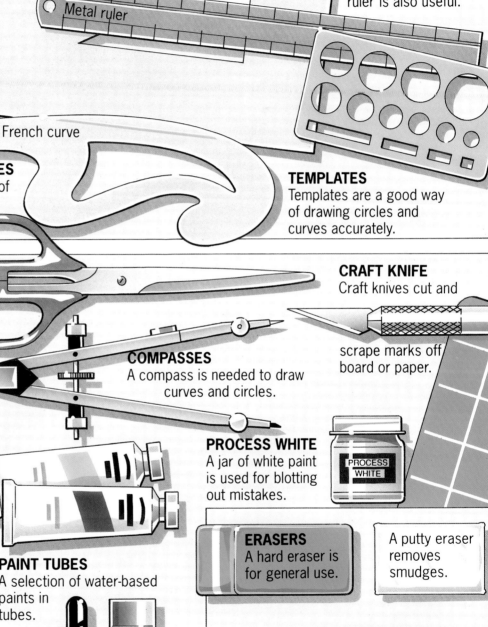

MASKING TAPE
An all-purpose tape that can be lifted and re-positioned.

CLEAR TAPE
Household tape is used to stick anything.

DOUBLE SIDED TAPE
This tape is not easy to re-position but is useful for neat presentation.

INVISIBLE TAPE
Useful for presentation and pasting-up work as it does not photocopy.

PLASTIC TAPE
Strong parcel tape doesn't come unstuck.

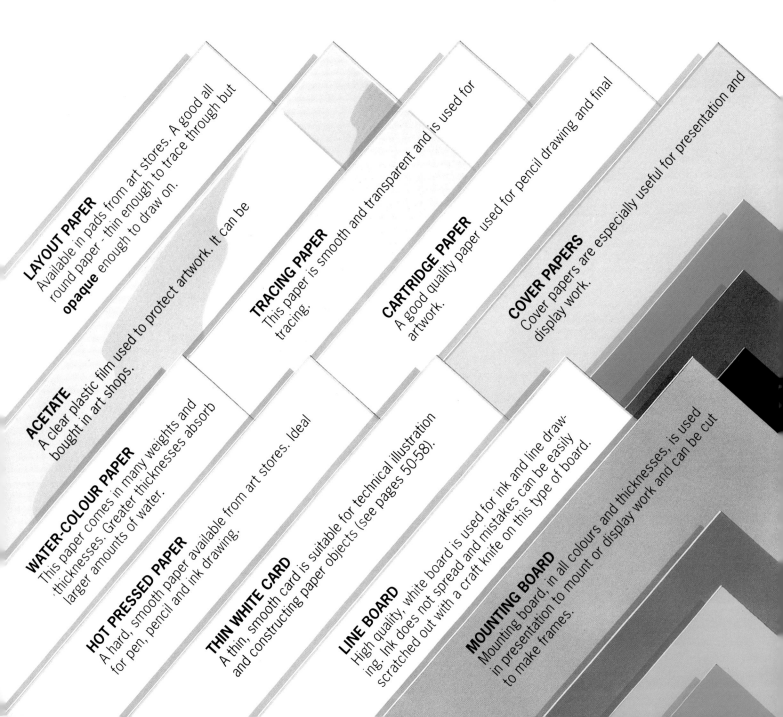

LAYOUT PAPER
Available in pads from art stores. A good all round paper - thin enough to trace through but **opaque** enough to draw on.

ACETATE
A clear plastic film used to protect artwork. It can be bought in art shops.

TRACING PAPER
This paper is smooth and transparent and is used for tracing.

CARTRIDGE PAPER
A good quality paper used for pencil drawing and final artwork.

COVER PAPERS
Cover papers are especially useful for presentation and display work.

WATER-COLOUR PAPER
This paper comes in many weights and thicknesses. Greater thicknesses absorb larger amounts of water.

HOT PRESSED PAPER
A hard, smooth paper available from art stores. Ideal for pen, pencil and ink drawing.

THIN WHITE CARD
A thin, smooth card is suitable for technical illustration and constructing paper objects (see pages 50-58).

LINE BOARD
High quality, white board is used for ink and line drawing. Ink does not spread and mistakes can be easily scratched out with a craft knife on this type of board.

MOUNTING BOARD
Mounting board, in all colours and thicknesses, is used in presentation to mount or display work and can be cut to make frames.

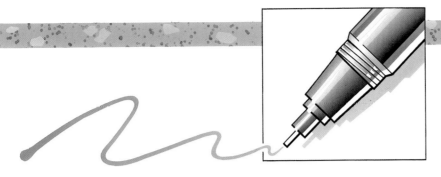

Chapter 2
Studio Skills and Techniques

TRAINING YOURSELF

Graphic designers work with words, pictures, shape and colour. The success or failure of their work depends on how all these things look when they are put together. Individual flair and imagination can count for a lot but they are not everything. It is impossible to rely on ability and talent alone. To be a good graphic designer you need a wide range of basic technical skills and all designers go through a period of practical training either in a design studio or at art college.

important to master. You will find everything a lot easier, and much more fun, if you can create your own little studio. It does not have to be a whole room, a small space will do. All you need is a well lit area (preferably with its own light source - a good table - or angle-poise lamp, for instance) with enough room for you to set up your drawing board and store your equipment and materials. In this way you can keep everything you need together and within easy reach.

* How to transfer images.
* Getting the best out of your graphic equipment.
* Different lettering and alphabets.
* How to put words and lettering together on a page.
* How everything fits together in a final paste-up.

YOUR OWN STUDIO

Graphic skills and techniques are particularly

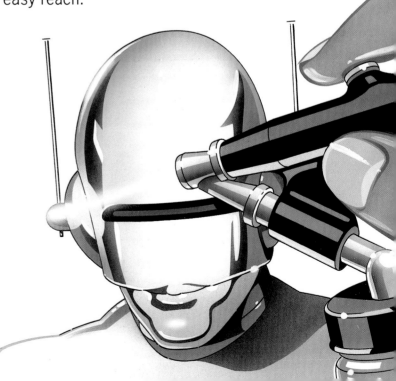

TRANSFERRING IMAGES

One of the first things a graphic artist learns to do is how to transfer images. You can save yourself a great deal of time and trouble, and create a much more professional effect, by finding and transferring existing images rather than trying to draw them yourself.

Original

Trace from an original picture.

Trace your image then transfer it on to your new background.

TRACING

Use a 2H pencil to trace an outline, scribble over the back of the paper with a soft pencil, then go over the outline with the hard pencil.

TRACING-DOWN PAPER

This paper is available from art shops. It has a special surface on one side and is inserted between the original, or your trace, and your paper. As you follow the outline, the tracing-down paper transfers the image on to the paper beneath it.

TRACING ON A WINDOW

Put your paper, tracing paper, and the image you wish to trace, up against a window. The extra light allows you to see finer details and makes the image easier to trace. To stop the paper slipping, secure it lightly with tape.

DESIGN TIP

Keep your drawings clean and smudge free. Wash your hands before starting work or if you get paint or ink on them. A piece of scrap paper under your hand stops you marking the paper.

USING A GRID

Images can be enlarged or reduced by using grids. Draw or trace a grid over the original and then lightly draw a matching grid on your paper, changing the size of the squares to make the image larger or smaller. Transfer exactly what you see in each section, using particular reference points to guide you, and build up the image box by box.

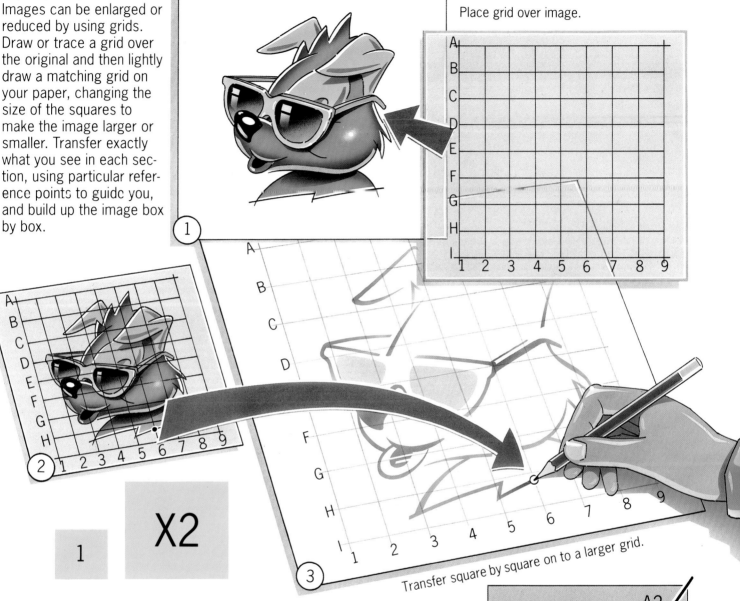

Place grid over image.

Transfer square by square on to a larger grid.

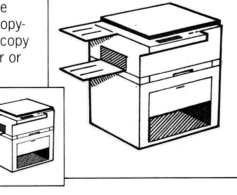

1

X2

ENLARGING IN PROPORTION

The easiest way to enlarge or reduce things in proportion is with a photocopying machine. Photocopiers not only copy images, they also make them bigger or smaller. The images are kept in proportion because the machines take standard A sized paper (see opposite). A diagonal line can be drawn through the corners of all the paper sizes, from the largest to the smallest, because each is in proportion to the one above and below it. As long as the image you wish to enlarge or reduce is on standard A sized paper, you can set up the machine to transfer the image and make it bigger or smaller.

A2

A3

A4

COMPASSES

Compasses make it possible to draw accurate arcs and circles. An ordinary compass is useful for drawing coloured circles as it can hold a crayon. If you are using a pencil, a **spring-bow** compass has the advantage of a locking device which allows the compass to repeat the circle without moving out of position. Some compassess are available with attachments for technical pens. Keep pencil leads sharpened with an **emery board** or **emery paper**.

CRAFT KNIVES

Straight-edged scalpels and craft knives are for cutting. Round-edged blades are used for scraping off marks. If you are not used to changing blades use a disposable knife. Cut against a metal ruler on a thick board or cutting mat. It is safest to use a knife with a bigger blade for thick card and paper. Apply even pressure to the knife when cutting and keep your fingers out of the way of the blade!

SET SQUARES AND LONG RULERS

Use a set square and a ruler to draw horizontal, vertical and angled lines. A 60 centimetre ruler is very useful. A bevelled (sloping) edge on a ruler prevents ink from pens, felt-tips or markers from seeping under the edge and spoiling the paper. Card or folded paper placed underneath the set square or ruler gives the same protection as a bevelled edge.

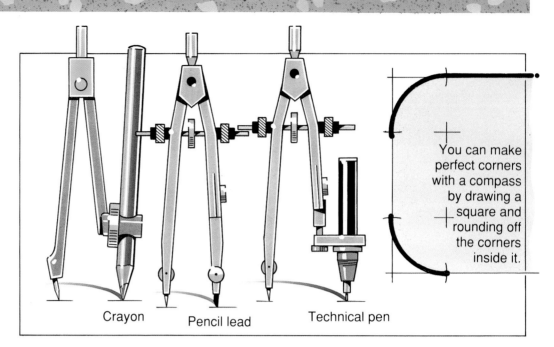

Crayon   Pencil lead   Technical pen

You can make perfect corners with a compass by drawing a square and rounding off the corners inside it.

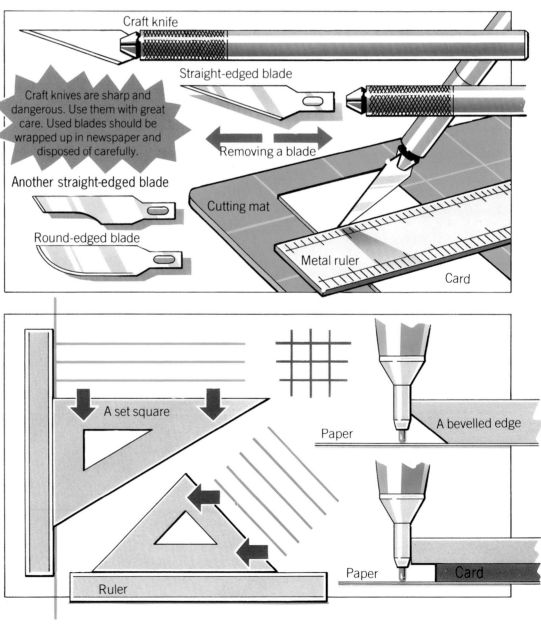

Craft knife

Straight-edged blade

Craft knives are sharp and dangerous. Use them with great care. Used blades should be wrapped up in newspaper and disposed of carefully.

Another straight-edged blade

Round-edged blade

Removing a blade

Cutting mat

Metal ruler

Card

A set square

Paper

A bevelled edge

Ruler

Paper   Card

TECHNICAL PENS

Technical pens are used for accurate, detailed artwork. Technical pens can be expensive, but to start with you only need a thick and thin one. Always remember to replace the top or else the pen will not last long. To draw perfect corners with a technical pen, overdraw the lines and then scrape away the extra ink with a craft knife. Alternatively you could hide the extra lines with white paint or process white.

MARKER PENS

The broad tip of a marker pen allows you to cover large areas with colour by applying quick, even strokes. At first, you do not need a wide range of colours - but black is essential, grey is useful, and you should have the basic primary colours of red, yellow and blue. If you want to draw a really straight edge put masking tape down over the edge and colour over it - then carefully remove the tape.

AIRBRUSHES

Airbrushes spray paint and ink on to paper and give strong or weak colours depending on how near to the paper they are held. As with marker pens (see above) use masking tape to draw a straight, clean line. A simple, single action airbrush is the model most suited to beginners and they can be found in all good art and model shops. You will also need to buy an aerosol propellant and an **air supply line**.

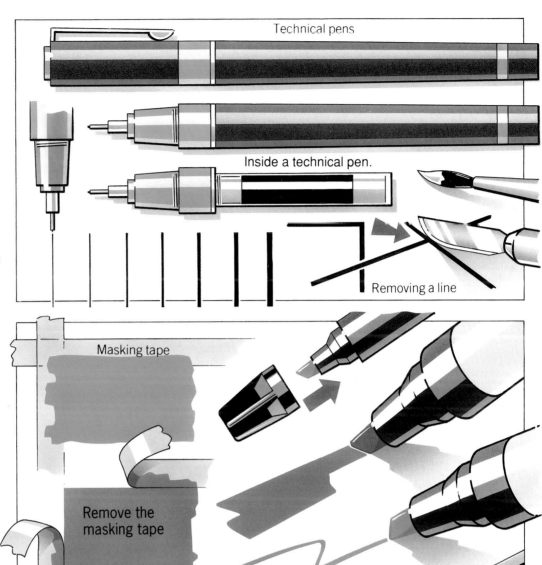

Technical pens

Inside a technical pen.

Removing a line

Masking tape

Remove the masking tape

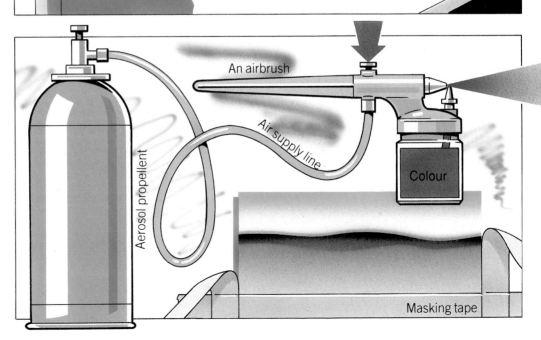

An airbrush

Aerosol propellent

Air supply line

Colour

Masking tape

LETTERING

Lettering is a very big subject. I only have space to show you a few of the many forms and types of lettering that it is possible to use. Here I will introduce the special terms used to describe lettering and show you some of the basic techniques that are used to make letters. There are also four alphabets for you to trace and transfer (opposite page). You can use the lettering in many of the design projects.

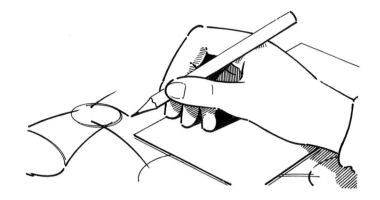

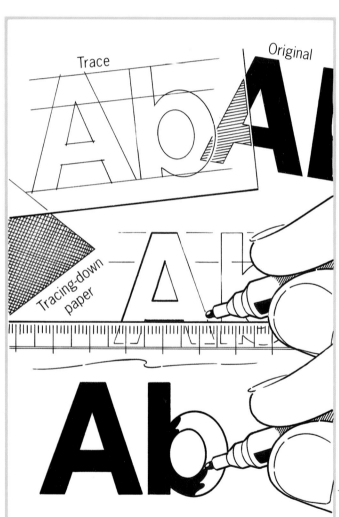

DESIGN TIP

Transferring letters by hand.
1. Draw your letter, using a 2H pencil and tracing-down paper.
2. Carefully draw the outline in ink, using a bevelled ruler.
3. Fill the letter in.

SERIFS
Serifs are the strokes which finish off the arms, stems and curves of letters.

SANS SERIF
Sans serif refers to letters or type which are without serifs.

CAPITALS - ROMAN
Capital (upper case) letters which are upright are called Roman.

CAPITALS - ITALIC
Capital (upper case) letters which are *slanted* are called italic.

LOWER CASE - ROMAN
Small (lower case) upright letters are called Roman

LOWER CASE - ITALIC
Small (lower case) *slanted* letters are called italic.

SERIF TEXT
Serif type is easier to read than sans serif as serifs make it easier to tell the letters apart.

SAN SERIF TEXT
Sans serif type is more difficult to read because the letters look more like each other when they do not have serifs.

AB ab

GH gh

NOPQ

LMNO

abcdef

abcde

TYPEFACES

Different styles of lettering are called typefaces. Designers vary their use of type-faces to convey different ideas and messages. Always try to chose a typeface that is appropriate to the subject you are illustrating.

1 This alphabet is called *Univers.* It is a sans serif typeface.

ABCDEFGHIJKLMNOPQRSTUVWXYZ
abcdefghijklmnopqrstuvwxyz
£1123456789O&(.,:;"!?-)

2 This alphabet is called *Times New Roman.* It is a serif typeface.

ABCDEFGHIJKLMNOPQRSTUVWXYZ
abcdefghijklmnopqrstuvwxyz
£1234567890&(.,:;"!?-)

3 This alphabet is called *One Stroke.* It is a script typeface. Script means that it looks like writing that has been done by hand.

ABCDEFGHIJKLMNOPQRSTUVWXYZ
abcdefghijklmnopqrstuvwxyz
£1234567890&(.,:;"!?-)

4 This alphabet is called *Futura Bold.*

ABCDEFGHIJKLMNOPQRSTUVWXYZ
abcdefghijklmnopqrstuvwxyz
£1234567890&(.,:;'""!?-)

Spacing is very important. Lettering or type that is not spaced properly is difficult to read and looks wrong.

LETTER SPACING

For lettering to look good, the gaps between the letters must all appear to be equal - even if they may not actually be so.

WORD SPACING

Spacing between words is important. Leave a space the size of a small 'n' between words made up of small letters and a space the size of a large 'O' between words in large letters.

LINE SPACING

Line spacing is the space between two lines of lettering or type. Generally, the longer the lines, the bigger the spacing!

DRY TRANSFER LETTERING

Dry transfer lettering is ideal for headings and short messages. Remember to line up each letter carefully. It is easier to use a **burnisher**.

Good	Bad
long shape usually one household	I t wa s usually could k e e p went o u t thro

Good	Bad
In this book you Vikings made and of their greatness. we can build up a We can look at	we canbuild up a Wecan look at their clothesthey wore. and read about their and goddesses.

Good	Bad
have Viking carved on it. are called runes. were invented 2,	'Kaulfr and Autir, erected this stone owned Gusnava.' Sometimes runes

Cafe

FREEHAND LETTERING

When writing letters freehand, it is easier to copy an existing alphabet. In pencil draw two lines to mark the top and bottom of the capital letters and a line for the top of the small letters.

Dry transfer lettering

MMMMMMMMNNN
NNNNNNNNNNN
OOOOOOOOPPPPP
RRRRRRRRRRRR

Cafe

STENCILLING

You can buy a ready made stencil or make your own from thin card by cutting out the letters with a craft knife. Brush paint or ink through the stencil with a stiff brush, taking care not to smudge the lettering when you lift the stencil.

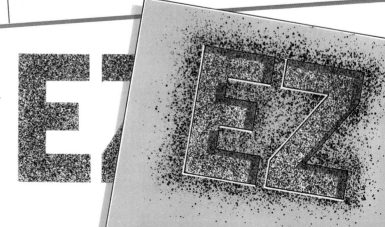

You may want to create your own text for a class magazine or a newsheet. The lettering, typing and printed material you collect to do this is called copy. Assembling the copy and putting it all together on a page is known as typesetting. Much of the printed material you see has been professionally typeset. But you can produce impressive, high quality, results of your own, if you have access to a typewriter or word processor and you are prepared to take a little time and trouble.

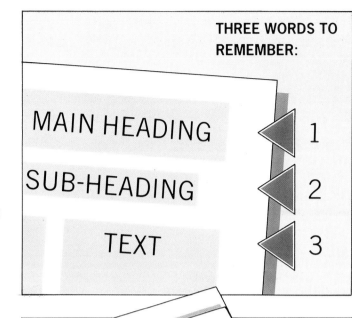

THREE WORDS TO REMEMBER:

MAIN HEADING — 1

SUB-HEADING — 2

TEXT — 3

DESIGN TIPS

* CAPITAL LETTERS take longer to read.

* Very long or very short lines are hard to read.

* Heavy type is called bold.

* Headings have the most impact when the first letter is a capital and the rest are small letters.

* It is best to have only one or two type styles in a design.

PROFESSIONAL TYPESETTING

If you need some type to be of a very high standard, you can send it to a professional typesetter. The typesetter follows all your instructions.

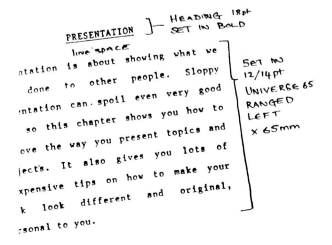

PRESENTATION] — HEADING 18pt SET IN BOLD

line space

ntation is about showing what we done to other people. Sloppy ntation can spoil even very good so this chapter shows you how to ove the way you present topics and jects. It also gives you lots of xpensive tips on how to make your k look different and original, rsonal to you.

SET IN 12/14pt UNIVERSE 65 RANGED LEFT x 65mm

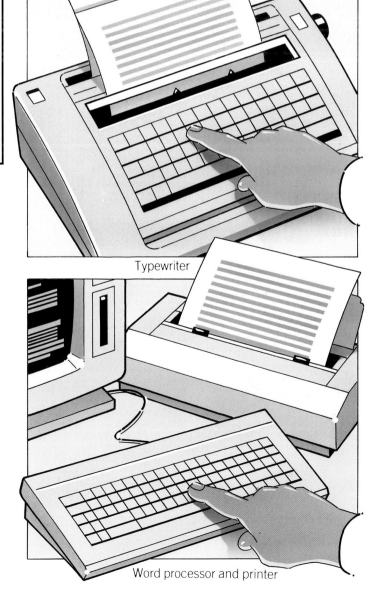

Typewriter

Word processor and printer

LAYOUT AND PASTE-UP

The way lettering, type, and pictures are organized on a page is called layout. Collecting and assembling all the components of the page and arranging them for final reproduction is called pasting-up. For paste-up you will need guidelines drawn in blue pencil on your paper. Tape the guides to your drawing board. You will find a T-square helps when marking the grid and to check that pieces of copy are straight. If you do not have a T-square use a long ruler.

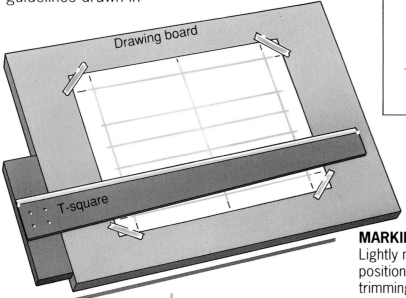

Drawing board

T-square

MARKING AND CUTTING

Lightly mark the lettering or text, to assist with correct positioning within your guidelines. Cut the text carefully, trimming to within 3mm of the edge. Draw trim marks round the edge of the whole page with a T-square or ruler in black ink. This border should be slightly bigger than the final page to prevent loss of copy. You can trim the page to the exact size later.

THREE STAGES OF PASTE-UP

[1]

Mark your page lightly to indicate where the lettering and pictures are to go.

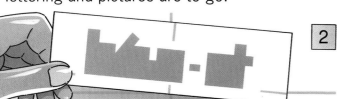

[2]

Check that everything fits. Apply adhesive to the back of each piece of copy.

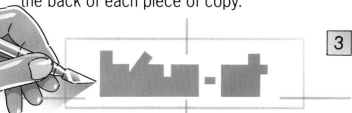

[3]

Position each piece carefully, using the marks you have made for guidance. Use a ruler to check that they are straight.

DESIGN TIP

Tape a sheet of thin, cheap paper to the back of any artwork you are working on. When you finish your work, or if you have to leave it for any reason, bring the sheet over the top to protect it.

Paper to cover work.

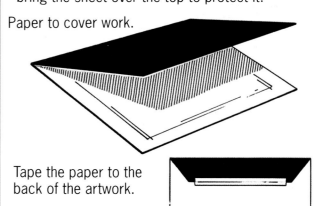

Tape the paper to the back of the artwork.

THE FINAL PASTE-UP

This page shows you how to combine some of the studio techniques you have learnt so far in a final paste-up.

1 A CLEAN SURFACE

Work on a flat, clean, uncluttered surface. Wash your hands before you start and take care not to smudge or spoil lettering, type or artwork.

2. BE SECURE

Fix the page you are working on with masking tape (this does not harm the paper). Make sure anything you need is within easy reach.

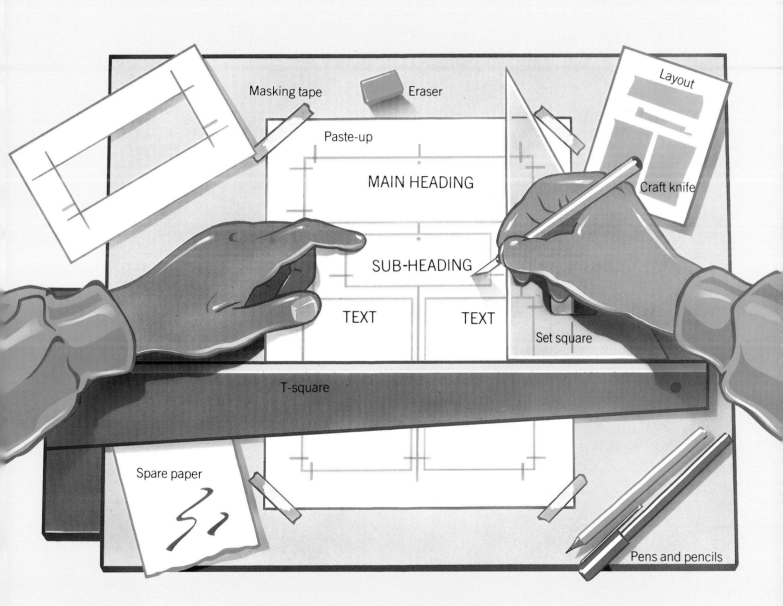

Masking tape

Eraser

Paste-up

Layout

MAIN HEADING

Craft knife

SUB-HEADING

TEXT   TEXT

Set square

T-square

Spare paper

Pens and pencils

3 GUIDELINES

Use a set square and ruler to draw guidelines in light blue pencil. Draw in the outside edges of the page and then any other guides you need.

4 THE WORDS

Lightly pencil-in where you will position the type. Mark the type so that you can match it up on the page. Handle it lightly and don't smudge it.

5 CUTTING

Cut out the type with a craft knife on a cutting mat or board. Apply the glue (spray glue or rubber cement so that it can be moved around) to the type.

6 LINE-UP

Position the type carefully, matching it up with the marks you have made as guides. Move it around, if necessary, with a craft knife or pencil.

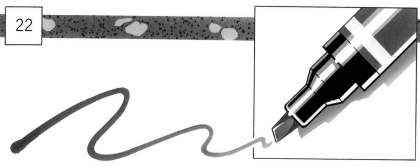

Chapter 3

Graphic Design

THERE HAS ALWAYS BEEN DESIGN

Graphic design is a basic human activity with a history as long as our own existence. Design is an art that is used for a purpose, whether by prehistoric men and women to ensure a good hunt and ward off evil spirits, or by modern businesses to sell their products and make them recognizable throughout the world. Without design much of our familiar world would become unrecognizable. We would not be able to function for long within such a bare environment.

COMMUNICATING WITH DESIGN

Graphic design communicates ideas through words and pictures. Some of the images created in this way are as familiar as the natural world around us or the faces of our family and friends. If we think of a well known product, it is often not just the name we see in our heads, it is the shape and colour of the words and letters. We remember the work of the graphic artist who designed the lettering for the brand name. Some products are so famous and successful that they are known throughout the world. Even in the remotest places people recognize the distinctive colour of the label and the shape of the letters that spell out the product's name.

FAMILIAR IMAGES

There are some signs and logos, like road signs, which need no language to explain what they refer to. The image the designer has created is recognized, everywhere, by everybody.

THINKING ABOUT DESIGN

We see examples of good graphic design all the time. They may appear to be casually put together with little effort but this is rarely the case. Although design projects start off in a very simple way: as an idea in someone's head and a few sketches on a piece of paper, a graphic

designer has to work out many things carefully and go through different stages before producing a satisfactory end result. From a multi-million pound advertising campaign, to a new magazine, to packaging for a new product, a film poster or the title sequence of a new television programme - all design projects begin with the designer being given a 'brief' by a **client** (see page 24).The client wants something designed, such as a book cover or a compact disc cover, and passes on ideas and instructions to the graphic designer who trys to **realize** these ideas in a way that will communicate them effectively.

EXPERIMENT!
The skills required from designers are many and diverse. Designers often specialize in particular areas of work but they all tend to approach projects in a similar way. After researching the subject they try out many ideas before deciding which one to use. Most importantly they are not afraid to experiment!

COLLECTING DESIGNS
You can learn a great deal about how graphic designers work from looking at their work. Learn to use your eyes. Look out for examples of good design in advertisements, magazines, book covers and packaging. Collect examples of design that you find interesting.

Use your eyes to judge each stage of your own work. If it looks good to you it will look good to others as well.

PRACTISING DESIGN
Graphic design is a very competitive industry and to succeed designers have to be hard working and self-motivated as there are many stages from the initial starting point to the final product. Good design is not just about having visually interesting ideas and using exciting graphic effects, you have to practice to acquire the skills you need. You will find, however, that the work is all worthwhile when you produce something which pleases you and is also admired by other people.

BE REALISTIC
The best results come from being careful and methodical. Don't be over-ambitious. Stick to what is realistic with the time, money and materials available to you. Real graphic designers have to keep to strict deadlines and budgets.

CREATING A UNIQUE DESIGN
When you have finished all the stages of creating your own design, you will have the excitement and satisfaction of knowing that what you have produced is unique. There is nothing else, anywhere, quite like it.

DIFFERENT STAGES IN A DESIGN

1 THE BRIEF

The client gives the designer a set of instructions (the brief) about what the design is for and how much it should cost.

2 RESEARCH/ IDEAS

The designer considers the brief and comes up with several ideas. You need to think about who and what the design is for. You can get ideas by doing research - looking at examples of similar things in shops, magazines and books.

3 ROUGHS AND MOCK-UPS

Try your ideas out in small, rough sketches. Rough work is vital for sorting out ideas. Arrange your roughs in different ways to see how they work. These are called mock-ups. The final mock-up is called the layout.

4 COST

Graphic designers work out exactly how much each job will cost. Even if you are not working for a paying client, it is still a good idea to have some idea of the cost of the finished work in terms of the materials you use.

5 ELEMENTS

Collect together all the different materials and sketches you have been working on. Lettering, photographs and pictures drawn up on separate paper are all called elements. An element is anything you need to complete your work.

6 ARTWORK/ LAYOUT

Complete your artwork according to your final layout (see roughs and mock-ups). On the card or paper you have selected, neatly transfer, trace-down or paste-up the lettering and pictures. Draw borders directly on to the artwork.

7 FINAL PRODUCTION

Review your final work to ensure that it fullfils the brief - for example, if you have made a card, do you have an envelope to go along with it?

VISUALS AND ROUGHS

Once you know what you want to achieve and have found out what information has to be included, work out your ideas visually as thumbnails (see below). Re-draw the best thumbnails as full sized roughs. You can add colour, make refinements, show people the design and get their opinion.

When you have decided on a design which is clear, looks good, and fulfils the brief, then you produce a 'visual'. This is a full sized, coloured-in, carefully worked out design which gives an idea of the finished work.

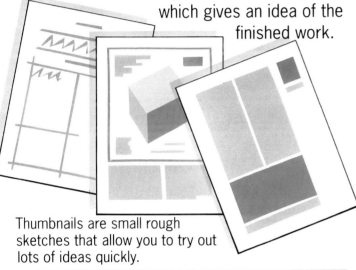

Thumbnails are small rough sketches that allow you to try out lots of ideas quickly.

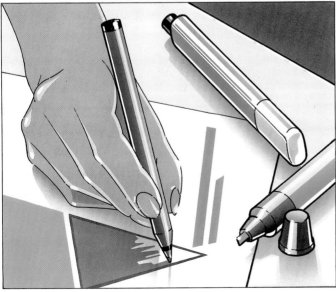

COLOUR
Add colour to roughs and visuals with felt tip pens and markers. Colour picks out particular features and helps you to imagine the final work.

MOCK-UP BOOKLET
If you want to make a booklet try out your design by putting together a mock-up (see below). A mock-up is a model of what you are making and it helps you to see what the final product will look like.

DESIGN TIP

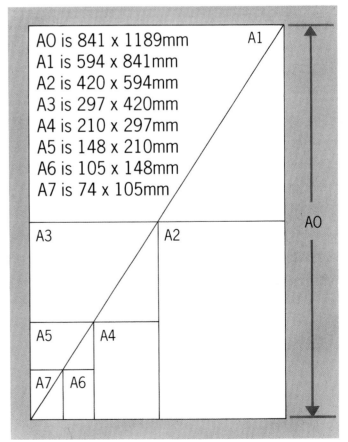

When you make a large booklet and need to staple the pages along the centre use your stapler in its open position. Put an eraser under the paper/card to receive the staples, and then bend the staple ends over with your metal ruler.

AO is 841 x 1189mm
A1 is 594 x 841mm
A2 is 420 x 594mm
A3 is 297 x 420mm
A4 is 210 x 297mm
A5 is 148 x 210mm
A6 is 105 x 148mm
A7 is 74 x 105mm

SIZE
You should always work with the international 'A' size series (above). Each A sheet is half the previous size, this helps to keep your work in proportion.

LAYOUT AND DESIGN

The first stage in any layout is to draw a grid. The grid is important because it is the frame within which you work and it keeps the page organized. A four column grid was used to design this book. As you look through it, notice how the invisible grid controls the way the pictures and text are organized on the pages. You will also see that you do not have to stick to the grid. Photographs and illustrations can spill across columns and this helps to make the book look more interesting.

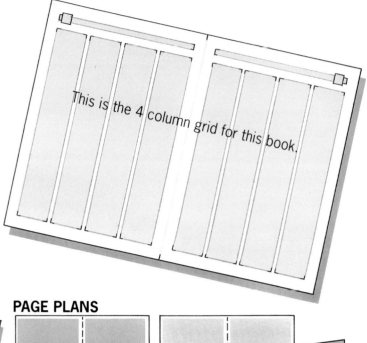
This is the 4 column grid for this book.

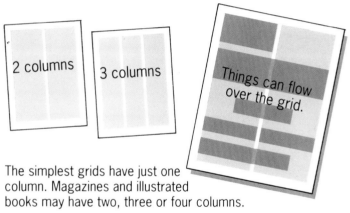

2 columns

3 columns

Things can flow over the grid.

The simplest grids have just one column. Magazines and illustrated books may have two, three or four columns.

PAGE PLANS

4 1   2 3   1

If you are designing a magazine or booklet remember to make a page plan so that the page numbers run consecutively when the whole thing is put together.

USING GRIDS

Once you have decided on the grid size, draw a master grid on a thin piece of card using a light blue pencil. Blue pencil will not show up when it is photocopied.

This master grid is the framework for the layout of the page and it will give a uniform look to the whole book. Trace and transfer the parts of the grid you need as you work.

Working design

First design

Trace

Grid

EXPERIMENT!

When you have decided on your basic grid, experiment with the elements of your design to see how they best fit into it. Crop photographs (see box opposite) and photocopy other material, making it bigger or smaller so that you can cut it out and move it around until you are satisfied. The same elements arranged in different ways can change the look of a page significantly. Examine each layout carefully and decide which is the most visually interesting.

Variations of layouts in this book.

DESIGN TIP

Cropping is the name given to cutting out the parts of a picture or photograph that you don't need. Cut two pieces of L-shaped card and use them to make rectangles. Move them until you have the size needed to frame the part of the picture or photograph that you want to use.

Play around with all the elements in your design.

DESIGN PROJECT 1: DESIGN A LOGO

A logo must :
* Project the right image
* Be simple and easy to reproduce
* Be instantly recognizable
* Be memorable
* Be equally effective at any size - from very small to very large, so it can be used on anything from business cards and labels to posters.

COMING UP WITH AN IDEA

I thought about the logos I have seen. The most successful ones have an immediate impact and are easy to recognize and remember. I thought of the equipment associated with graphic design and the items designers use and decided to use a pencil as a symbol of the designer. Pencils are used all the time, they are instantly recognizable and easy to draw. A realistic drawing of a pencil would not be very interesting so I tried to draw it in different ways and I came up with something smaller, chunkier and more interesting for use as a logo than a 'real' pencil shape.

1 THE BRIEF

The brief is to design a logo for a graphic designer.

I have chosen one particular design to show you the stages to go through. You may adapt this logo for your own use or design another one if you want to.

Look for inspiration in books, magazines and art galleries.

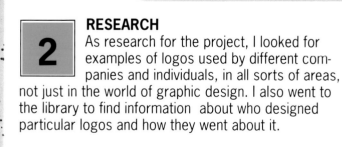

2 RESEARCH

As research for the project, I looked for examples of logos used by different companies and individuals, in all sorts of areas, not just in the world of graphic design. I also went to the library to find information about who designed particular logos and how they went about it.

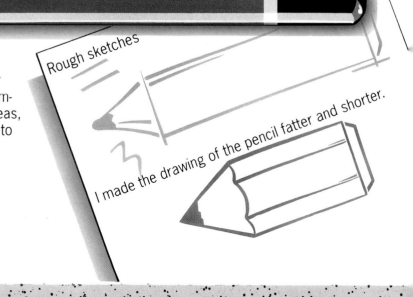

Rough sketches

I made the drawing of the pencil fatter and shorter.

ROUGHS

3

I drew the pencil shape and then decided the design would have more impact if the pencil had a shadow behind it (known as a drop shadow) to make it look as though it lifts off the page. This was done by tracing the final shape, tracing it down once and then moving the tracing paper slightly and tracing it down again. I moved the image around, put it in a frame and finally added on a squiggle going out of the border to make it look as though the pencil is in use.

Make a tracing of the pencil and move it slightly to create the shadow.

Experimenting with rough ideas and sketches.

HOW TO PRODUCE THE WORK

4

The final artwork should be done in black and white, on A4 sized paper - so that the size can easily be enlarged or reduced by using a photocopier (see page 13). Any colouring can be done later. I decided not to put the flash in the master artwork but to add it by hand each time, perhaps in different colours, to give an individual feel to each logo.

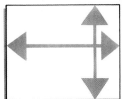

Before producing an image draw a rough of it to plan how it will look when it is enarged or reduced.

Adding the flash in colour later.

5 ELEMENTS

There are three elements that make up the final artwork - the flash, the pencil, and the framing box. I drew each of these separately and then brought all of the individual tracings together and moved them around to create the final image. When I thought I had the right effect, I traced down the final logo on another sheet of tracing paper. This is called the master copy.

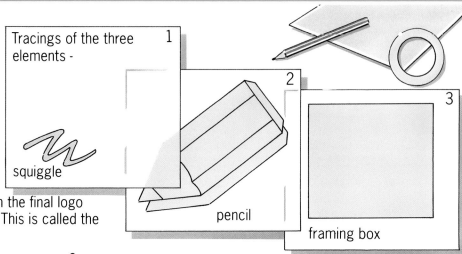

Tracings of the three elements -

1

squiggle

2

pencil

3

framing box

1

2

3

6 FINAL ARTWORK

Art board or paper that has a smooth, hard, white surface is best for the final stage as you need high quality materials for finished artwork. I carefully traced-down the final image and then went over it again using a set square, ruler and technical pen.

Words and initial letters are also used for logos. Invent your own personal symbol, or use the letters of your name or initials, to invent your own logo. You can use your logo in a small format to add to your work or you can enlarge it and have tee-shirts and posters printed.

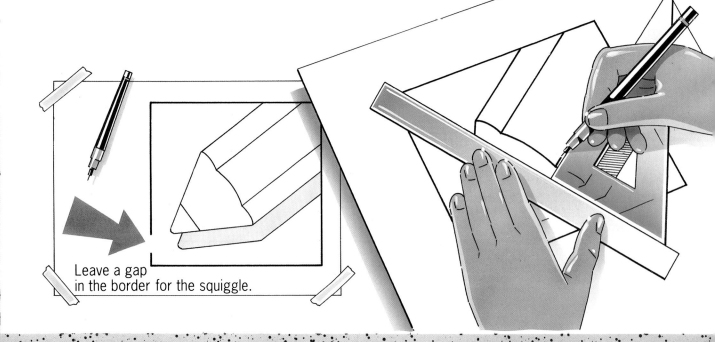

Leave a gap in the border for the squiggle.

7 FINAL PRODUCTION

The master artwork can be used to make many copies of the logo. It is in black and white so it will photocopy well. Once the number and size of the copies has been decided, the copies can be made, any colouring done and the final flashes added in selected colours.

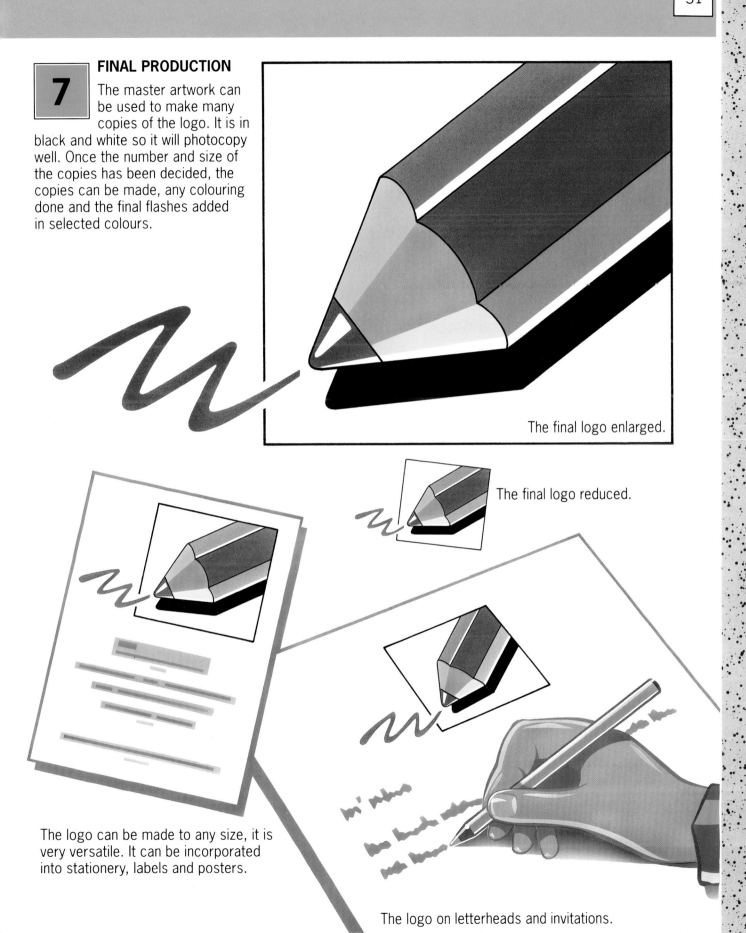

The final logo enlarged.

The final logo reduced.

The logo can be made to any size, it is very versatile. It can be incorporated into stationery, labels and posters.

The logo on letterheads and invitations.

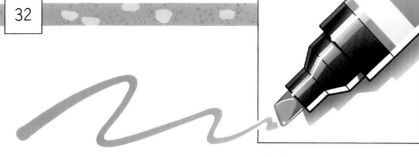

Chapter 4
Presentation

Presentation is about showing what we have done to other people. Smart presentation not only shows off your work, it says something about you too. Poor presentation can spoil even very good artwork.

WHY?
There are sound practical reasons for presenting work properly. By mounting artwork, you are not only more likely to create a good impression, you are also doing justice to your hours of hard work.

BE PRACTICAL
Placing work in a folder or portfolio makes transportation much easier and stops the work getting dog-eared and damaged. Covering artwork with a transparent sheet or acetate helps to protect it from dirt, finger smudges and accidental marking. Folders and carrying cases are useful for protecting work, especially when travelling. These cases also keep work safe, clean and organized. Plastic display folders are useful when presenting and displaying work because they allow people to see at a glance what you have done.

BEING DISTINCTIVE
You can incorporate your own label or logo into folders, to make your work recognizable.

DESIGN TIPS
* Cover your artwork to protect it from dirt and damage.
* Personalize covers and folders with your own label or logo.
* Mount your artwork to set it off and create a better impression.
* Photograph or photocopy all your finished work.
* Keep copies of work you have done in a personal record folder.

Zoom tube

USEFUL EQUIPMENT
Plastic display folders are useful when presenting and displaying work. They allow people to see at a glance what you have done.

Plastic display folder

Folder

Art cases are the same as portfolios but more expensive. They tend to be used by professional artists and designers. Plastic cases are cheap and smart. Their

Ring-binder folders keep notes in order and can also be used to present written projects. Some large artwork is easily damaged (like posters) and is best rolled and carried in a **zoom tube**.

Art case

Ring-binder

Your artwork should be kept in a portfolio large enough to take the larger sizes of art board and paper. Plastic or card portfolios are inexpensive and invaluable for storing and transporting artwork and displaying your work to other people.

Folders and carrying cases are important to protect work, especially in transit, and to keep it safe, clean and organized.

See pages 54-55 for instructions on how to make a document folder.

Portfolio

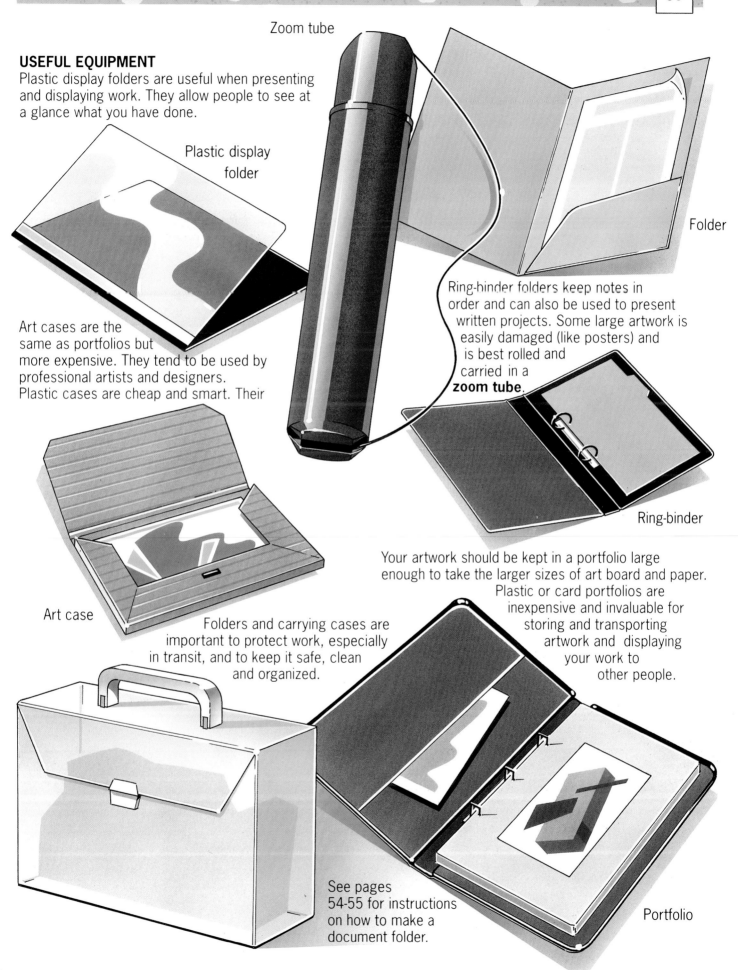

MOUNTING AND COVERING ARTWORK

Mount and cover your artwork, especially illustrations. A mount strengthens your work. A cover provides protection. When mounting work remember to make the bottom border slightly wider to give a visual balance.

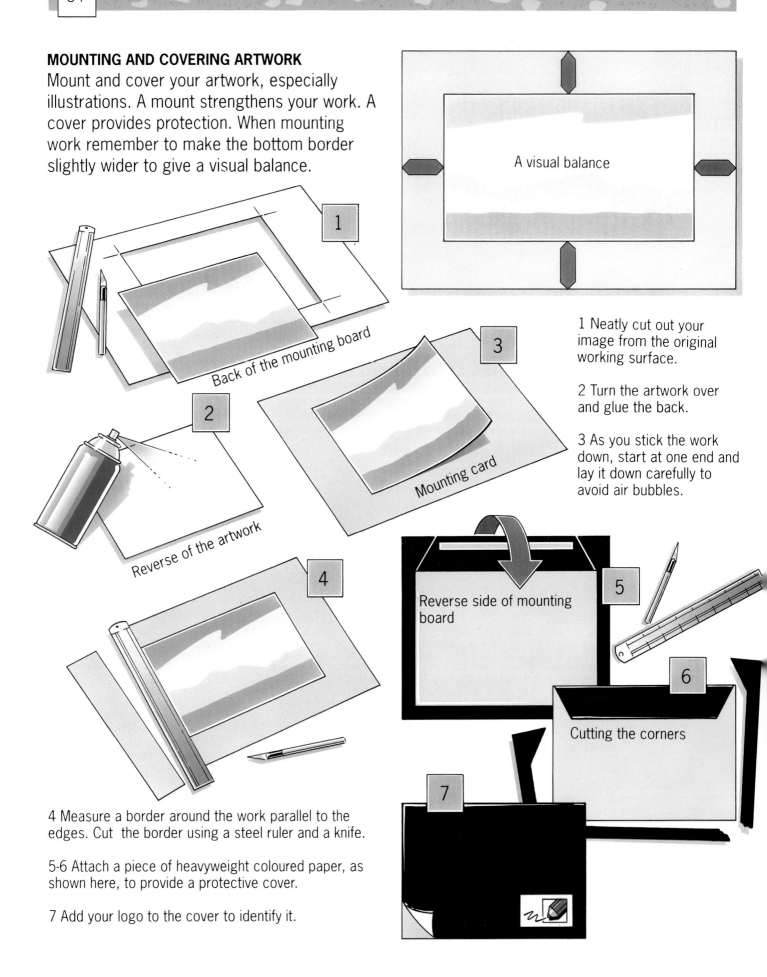

A visual balance

Back of the mounting board

Reverse of the artwork

Mounting card

Reverse side of mounting board

Cutting the corners

1 Neatly cut out your image from the original working surface.

2 Turn the artwork over and glue the back.

3 As you stick the work down, start at one end and lay it down carefully to avoid air bubbles.

4 Measure a border around the work parallel to the edges. Cut the border using a steel ruler and a knife.

5-6 Attach a piece of heavyweight coloured paper, as shown here, to provide a protective cover.

7 Add your logo to the cover to identify it.

WINDOW MOUNTS

A window mount, as the name suggests, is a piece of card or board with a space cut into it to make a window for your artwork. The artwork, often covered by a clear sheet of acetate, is then stuck to the frame.

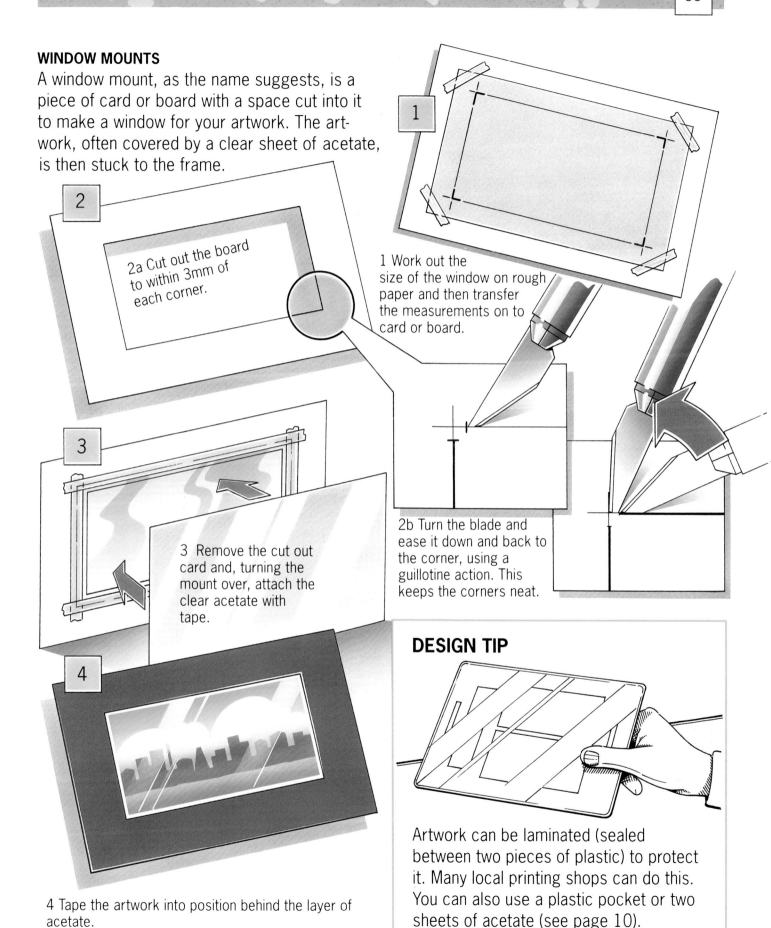

1 Work out the size of the window on rough paper and then transfer the measurements on to card or board.

2a Cut out the board to within 3mm of each corner.

2b Turn the blade and ease it down and back to the corner, using a guillotine action. This keeps the corners neat.

3 Remove the cut out card and, turning the mount over, attach the clear acetate with tape.

4 Tape the artwork into position behind the layer of acetate.

DESIGN TIP

Artwork can be laminated (sealed between two pieces of plastic) to protect it. Many local printing shops can do this. You can also use a plastic pocket or two sheets of acetate (see page 10).

DESIGN PROJECT 2 : PRESENTING WRITTEN WORK

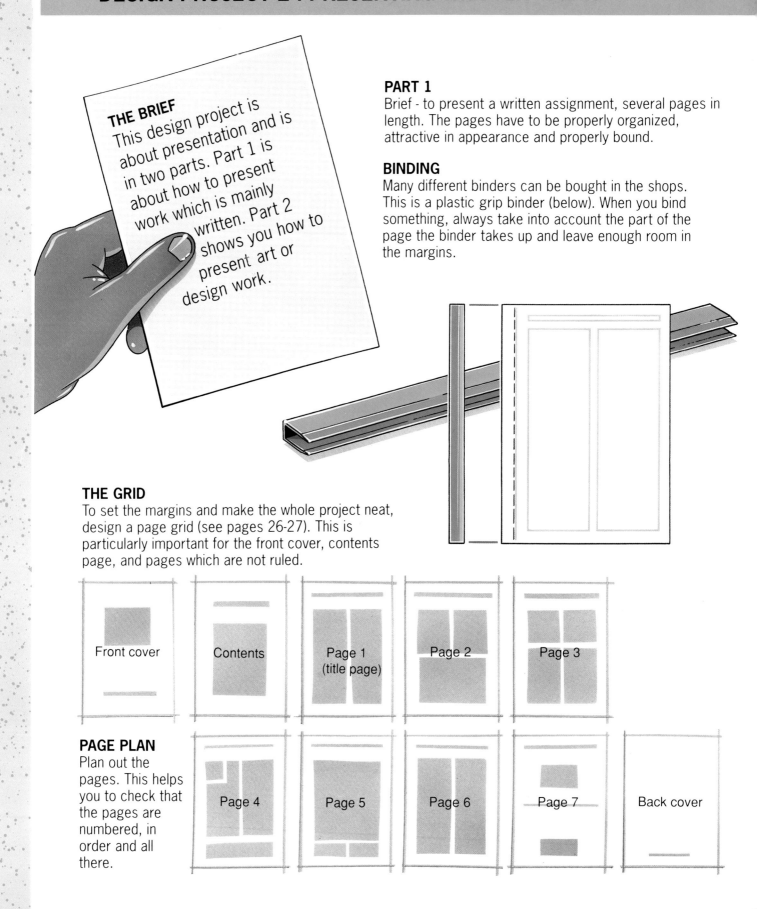

THE BRIEF
This design project is about presentation and is in two parts. Part 1 is about how to present work which is mainly written. Part 2 shows you how to present art or design work.

PART 1
Brief - to present a written assignment, several pages in length. The pages have to be properly organized, attractive in appearance and properly bound.

BINDING
Many different binders can be bought in the shops. This is a plastic grip binder (below). When you bind something, always take into account the part of the page the binder takes up and leave enough room in the margins.

THE GRID
To set the margins and make the whole project neat, design a page grid (see pages 26-27). This is particularly important for the front cover, contents page, and pages which are not ruled.

Front cover

Contents

Page 1 (title page)

Page 2

Page 3

PAGE PLAN
Plan out the pages. This helps you to check that the pages are numbered, in order and all there.

Page 4

Page 5

Page 6

Page 7

Back cover

DESIGN TIPS
* Make sure the pages are numbered.
* Make sure you have included: contents page, back cover and title page or front cover.
* Include any special notes or acknowledgements.
* Copy your work for your personal record.

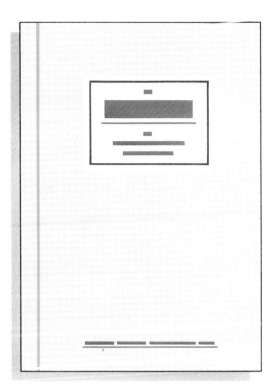

For the front cover, use coloured paper then glue on a different coloured title panel.

FRONT COVER
The front cover is what people see first. Apply what you have learnt in this book and your imagination to make your cover attractive and interesting. Use a light-coloured, thin card and use the same card for a plain, matching back cover.

FINAL PRODUCTION
Collect and square-up all the pages and the front and back covers. Make sure everything is in the correct order. Before you apply the grip binder, insert clear acetate between the cover and binder both back and front. This helps to protect your work while it is being read and gives it a professional finish.

The brief is to prepare your collection of art and design work for public display and presentation. Your work may be of different shapes and sizes but you should try to show eveything in a way that allows it to be seen as one complete body of work.

DESIGN TIPS
 * The work must be presented as a whole, not as a collection of bits and pieces.
 * Each piece of work should be mounted on card or board which is of the same size, colour and thickness.
 * If you cannot find the right colour, it is best, as a general rule, to use black.
 * Position the work carefully, remembering to balance the borders.

LOGO
Stick a label with your own logo or your name to each piece of work. The labels should be properly produced so that they do not detract from the quality of your artwork.

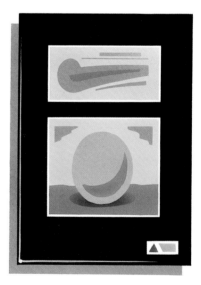

The mounting boards are all the same size. This gives a look of order to work of any size.

A plastic art case is essential if you are going to take your work anywhere and protect it properly. Art and design pieces tend to be large and difficult to carry. There is no other way of transporting them successfully. Your art case is very valuable. The work within represents many hours of effort. The case should be clearly labelled with your name, address and telephone number.

MAKE A STAND

If you have a piece of work which you would like to display then make a stand for the mount. When you have finished, the stand can fold flat and the work can be returned to your case.

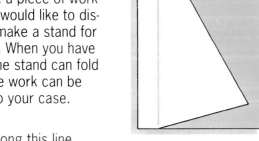

1 Cut this shape from thin card.

2 Score along this line

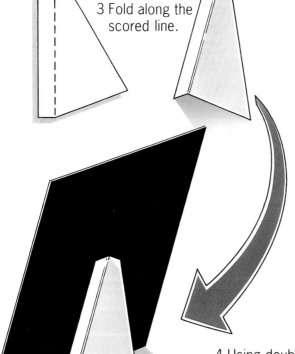

3 Fold along the scored line.

4 Using double-sided tape, apply to the back of the mount.

FIXING A LABEL

Art cases can receive some hard treatment so you need a way of fixing a secure label.
* Cover the front of the label with clear adhesive film, this makes it waterproof. Trim it neatly.
* Attach double-sided tape to the back of your label.
* Strip off the backing from the double-sided tape and stick it on to the case.
* Clear plastic film is useful for covering any kind of label but do not use it on top of artwork as it cannot be removed.

Chapter 5

Illustration

Illustrations are images associated with words. Some of the most famous illustrated books survive from medieval times (AD 476-1400) when few people could read. The books written then are called illuminated manuscripts. The illustrations they contained illuminated (cast light on) the text, so that people could follow the story even if they could not understand what was written on the page.

communicate information. This book is an illustrated book. Pictures and words work together to help you understand more about graphic design. Without the illustrations it would take many more words to explain even the simplest process.

Some illustrations appear to be just decorative and entertaining, but they often have a serious purpose underneath their surface attractiveness. Cartoons make us laugh, but they often make us think as well and we are more likely to attend an event if it is advertised by an exciting, eye-catching poster.

DESIGN TIPS
* Illustrators use many different **media**: pen and ink, pencil and crayon, **gouache**, oil paint, **acrylic** and water-colour.
* A basic knowledge of drawing is of help to an illustrator.
* Knowing a little about perspective is also useful in illustration.
* Observe subjects for illustration carefully.
* Collect your own library of reference material.

PICTURES GIVE INFORMATION
Whether the words explain the images or the images are there to help you understand the text, the main purpose of a book is to

REFERENCE

Just as, historically, artists paid models to pose for them, designers and illustrators working today need visual reminders of what an object looks like if they are to draw it accurately. The pictures they collect and copy, trace from, or use as background are called reference material. Good sources of reference material are: books, magazines, mail order catalogues and brochures.

COLLECTING PICTURES

Collect your own reference material - if you see a good picture of something you are interested in, keep it and store it. You can also take your own photographs of whatever it is you want to draw or use.

BASIC PERSPECTIVE

You should use perspective to help you to draw objects or buildings in a realistic way. Perspective plays an important part in any drawing or illustration. Here are a few rules (the vanishing point is always shown in pink).

THREE-POINT PERSPECTIVE - DOWNWARDS

The vertical and horizontal lines converge downwards to give a bird's eye view of objects from above.

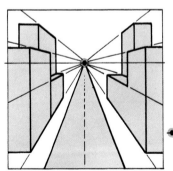

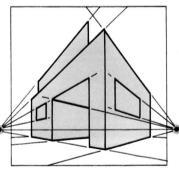

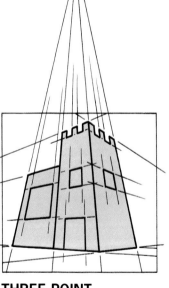

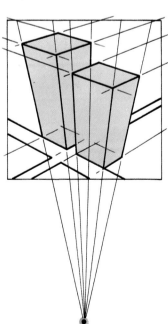

ONE-POINT PERSPECTIVE

The simplest perspective is used for head-on views. Horizontal lines **recede** from the object to meet at a point on the **horizon** called the vanishing point.

TWO-POINT PERSPECTIVE

This is used to draw objects at an angle. Two vanishing points on the horizon line meet from the nearest vertical line of the object.

THREE-POINT PERSPECTIVE - UPWARDS

In this form of perspective the vertical as well as the horizontal lines converge upwards, giving a worm's-eye view of an object from below.

LINE AND INK

Drawing with ink allows you to show clear detail and perspective in technical drawing and illustration. This technique communicates exact information about an object. Illustrators add shadow and tone to line drawings with dots, dashes, hatching and cross-hatching.

DESIGN TIPS

* A wide variety of pens can be used ranging from the traditional **quill** and steel nib to technical and fountain pens.
* The paper must be of a high quality with a hard **non-porous** surface.
* Use black, non-clogging ink for line drawing. **Indian ink** gives a deep black mark but takes longer to dry.
* For technical illustrations, a set of technical drawing instruments is essential.
* Coloured inks can be used to add washes after the ink outline has dried.

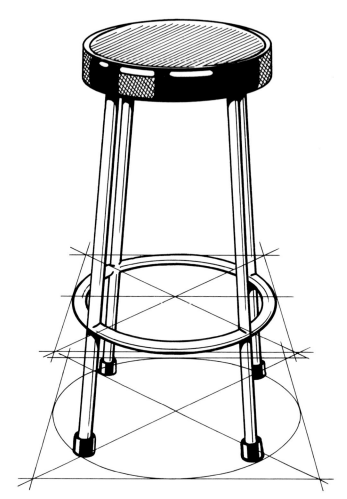

PAINTS

Illustrators use a variety of paints for different purposes. Their choice of paint depends on the effect they wish to create.

DESIGN TIPS

* Gouache paints are more opaque than water-colours and give flat areas of bright, solid colour.
*Water-colour's delicacy of tone and its variety and subtlety make it useful for **naturalistic** and atmospheric effects.
* Oil paints and acrylic paints are similar in their versatility and the sort of illustrations for which they can be used, but acrylic has the advantage of a faster drying time.

PENCIL/CRAYON

Pencil points can be used to make a variety of marks, from dots to **graduated lines**. Many different effects can be achieved by changes of pressure. Hard pencils are used to outline, softer grades are used for toning, either by cross-hatching or smudging to give a smooth, soft effect. Coloured pencils (crayons) can be used in the same way as graphite pencils. They are harder than chalks or pastels and can create subtle effects and strong, clear, often very realistic, images.

DESIGN TIPS
* You need a range of graphite pencils in different hardnesses.
* Pencil looks good on slightly rough paper.
* Soft erasers avoid damaging the paper.
* Mix colours by shading or cross-hatching one on top of another.

AIRBRUSH

In an airbrush, air under pressure is passed over ink or paint. This pressure **atomizes** the liquid and creates a fine, even spray. Professional artists use sophisticated airbrushes to create images as realistic as photographs.

DESIGN TIPS
* Ink, water-colour, gouache and acrylic can all be used in airbrushes.
* Clean the **paint reservoir** with each colour change.
* Use light textured paper or board.
* When covering large areas of colour keep the airbrush moving all the time.
* Do not spray too close to the paper or the paint will form puddles.

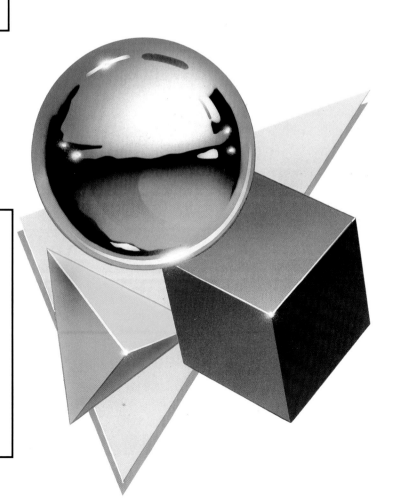

CARTOONS

Cartoons are a popular area of illustration but cartoon drawing is not as easy as it looks. A good way to get started is to copy cartoons drawn by other people before trying out your own ideas. Train yourself to notice the essential details of a subject and put them into your drawing.

* Drawing good faces is important as they communicate moods and character. A few simple lines and dots can make an expressive cartoon face.

* Hands can be drawn very simply and can show a great deal about a character and the story.

* To draw figures well it helps to have a basic knowledge of the proportions of the human body.

* Legs can tell us about a character and are often used to create a comic effect.

* Movements can be exaggerated and reinforced by the addition of movement lines.

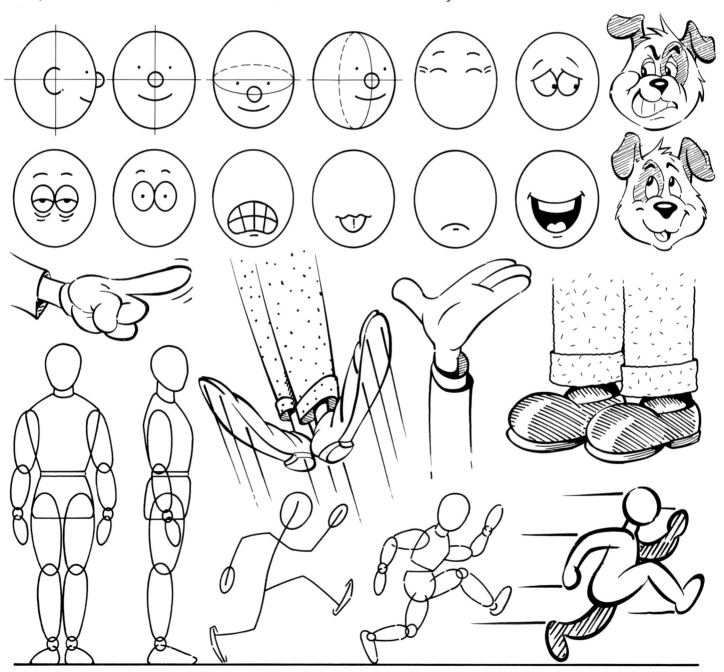

SUBJECT AND STYLE

When selecting a subject for illustration, you must choose the way it is to be drawn very carefully. You must not only consider the subject matter but also what the illustration will be used for. These factors will influence the technique and materials you use. The same subject can be made to look very different when executed in different ways with different equipment. Look at the difference in the way the head of this young woman (below) can be drawn. Different styles of illustration make the image more versatile.

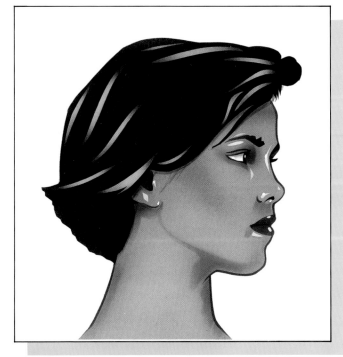

DESIGN PROJECT 3: DESIGN A POSTER

THE BRIEF

The brief is to design and produce a poster for a disco.

Before you start work on a brief, check that you understand exactly what it involves. Think about the purpose of this poster and the audience it is intended for. The poster has to be attractive and eye-catching but it also has to communicate specific information.

IDEAS & RESEARCH

Research helps you to sort out your ideas and decide how to proceed. Publicity posters are big, at least A3 size, but we will be using the A4 size for ease of working - this means our artwork will have to be enlarged - so we must work in proportion. The master artwork will be black and white so that posters can be printed on different colours of paper and the master used again.

THUMBNAILS

Doing thumbnails and roughs will give you the three elements that will make up the poster: lettering, illustration and information.

REFERENCE

Look for attractive, interesting references for the lettering in magazines, newspapers and on packaging.

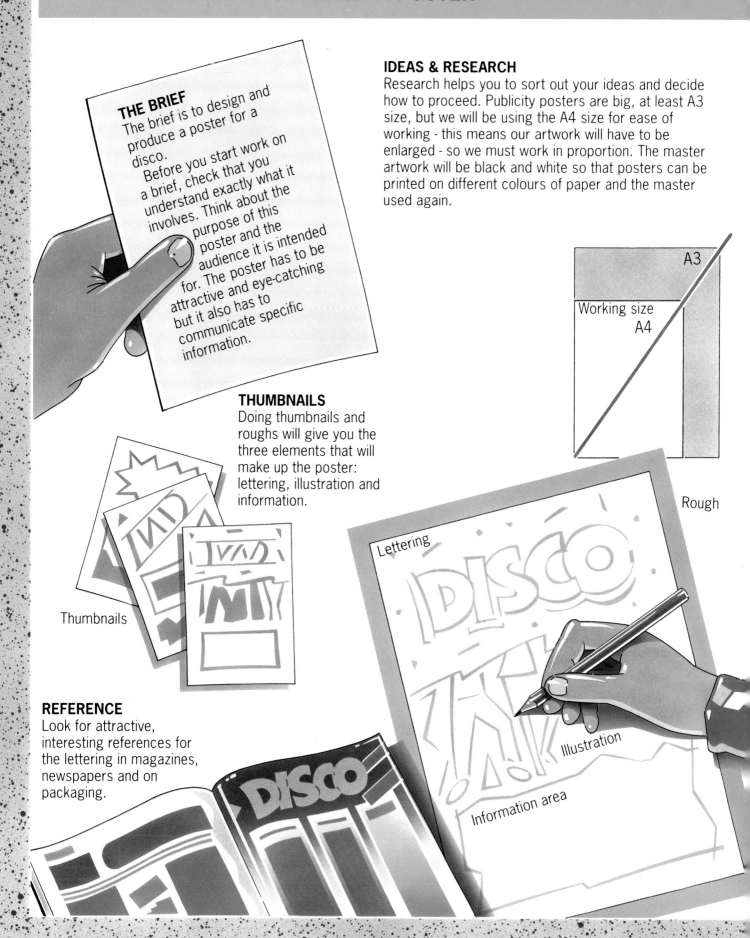

A3

Working size A4

Rough

Lettering

Illustration

Information area

Thumbnails

DISCO

1

Carefully trace the letters you have chosen from your reference material in order to make up the word 'Disco'.

Take another piece of tracing paper (or tracing-down paper) and play around with the letters until you are happy with what they look like. In this instance I have moved all the letters closer together so that they almost run into each other.

2

Draw an outline around the shape of the word with a sharp pencil. Use a ruler for the straight edges and to measure an equal distance from the letters for the outline.

3

4

5

Trace the outlined word once more so that you can create a drop shadow - the drop shadow makes the word look more energetic.

Go over the word with a black ink technical pen. Colour in the drop shadow. Draw another line underneath the word to separate it from the illustration you are about to put below.

ILLUSTRATION
References for the illustration which will appear under the lettering can be found in magazines and catalogues.

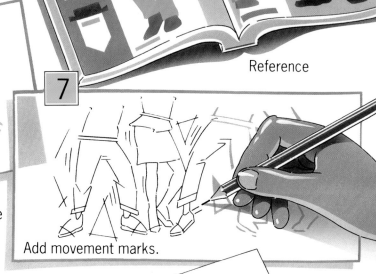
Reference

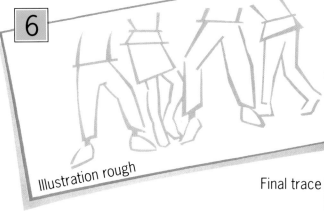

6

Illustration rough

7

Final trace

Add movement marks.

THE THREE ELEMENTS

Lettering

Image

8

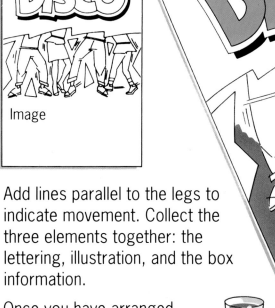

Colour in the final photocopied poster.

Information

Add lines parallel to the legs to indicate movement. Collect the three elements together: the lettering, illustration, and the box information.

Once you have arranged everything in a layout trace-down all the elements and go over the poster in technical pen.

INFORMATION BOX
You must always remember to leave enough room to put in information relevant to the poster or invitation. Essentials include:

Date:
Time:
Place:
Entrance charge:

The final product

Chapter 6

Card Engineering

Nearly everything we see in the shops is encased in packaging and presented in a way that is designed to invite us to buy. Some of the most common materials used in packaging are card and paper. Constructing packs and wrappers is called paper and card engineering.

Cartons, boxes, envelopes and folders, pop-up books, cards and display stands are all examples of card and paper engineering. They all started the same way - as a flat sheet of paper or cardboard - which then had to be measured, cut, creased, folded and stuck together to form the final three-dimensional object.

CARD ENGINEERING IS EVERYWHERE

If you look carefully at many of the things we take for granted you will start to see just how common and versatile card objects are. Envelopes that keep our letters safe and their contents confidential; the box that contains our morning breakfast cereal; the milk carton, sturdy and leakproof, that everyone can open, and so on. Take one of these familiar objects apart and see how it was put together; you will find that the construction is not as simple as it might seem at first.

DESIGN TIPS
* Look out for interesting or unusual examples of card engineering.
* Take different shaped (empty) boxes and cartons apart carefully.
* Work out how the boxes were cut from the original card and put together.
* Practise your cutting, folding and measuring skills on simple envelopes and folders.

BEING EXACT

Precision of measurement and accuracy has to be the same in paper and card as in any other area of engineering. Any mistakes in your planning and measuring will become obvious as the card is cut and constructed. A millimetre or two here and there can and will make all the difference between success and failure.

Packaging

Leaflet dispenser

STEP BY STEP

Working through each part of the process carefully and following the instructions exactly is the only way to make sure that the sides of a box or folder will line up and that any flaps and tucks will fit in snugly. Paper engineering can also be purely decorative, as in the Japanese paper folding art of **origami**.

Stationary

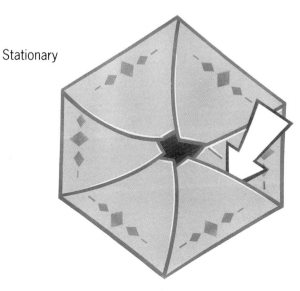

Display stand

MATERIALS

The paper, card or board you use may well determine whether your project succeeds or fails. You must choose the right material and make sure that it is strong enough.

PAPER WEIGHTS

Paper comes in different weights. These weights are measured in grams per square metre. The heavier the weight, the higher the number, 100 g/m² paper is lighter than 225 g/m² and so on. Board is referred to in terms of thickness (measured in mllimetres).

GRAIN

Paper and card are made of fibres. These fibres all lie in one direction and this is called the 'grain'. Paper and card folds and creases more smoothly in the direction of the grain. To test which way the grain runs, fold a test area of paper in both directions. The fold in the direction of the grain produces a crisp sharp fold. If you fold against the grain you will get an uneven ragged edge.

Test for grain in board or card by bending it one way and then turning it round and bending it the other way: it will bend more easily in the direction of the grain.

TOOLS

You will need a compass, ruler and T-square for accurate marking. A scalpel, craft knife, metal ruler and cutting mat are needed for cutting. Make sure you choose the correct cutting instrument for the weight of paper or board. A good pair of paper scissors is a sensible investment and a small roller is useful for flattening and smoothing creases.

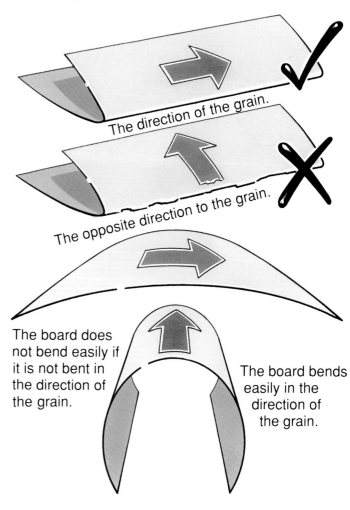

The direction of the grain.

The opposite direction to the grain.

The board does not bend easily if it is not bent in the direction of the grain.

The board bends easily in the direction of the grain.

Craft knife

Roller

Metal ruler

Cutting mat

Paper

Warning! Always be careful with your craft knife. Do not cut too deeply into the paper or card if you want to fold or crease it.

CREASING

All the creases and folds you make should have crisp, sharp edges. Folding paper or card by hand is not accurate enough: the surface breaks along the fold and the edge is untidy and ragged. You have to crease the paper surface first so that it will fold in the way you want it to. Make the crease by ruling along the line of the fold with a ball-point pen that has run out of ink. This invisible line makes a ridge along which the paper can be easily folded.

PERFORATING

Perforating means making a series of small cuts. These cuts release the tension in the paper or card, so that it folds more easily. Make sure the first and last cut are not too near the edges to avoid the risk of tearing.

CUTTING

Always be careful when cutting with a scalpel or craft knife. A sharp blade is essential. You should always have a supply of new, spare knife blades to hand. Use a metal ruler on a cutting mat or spare piece of board or card.

SCORING

Heavyweight card and board has to be scored before it is folded. Make a cut with a craft knife or scissor edge where you want the board to fold. Cut carefully. If the cut is too deep the card may break when handled.

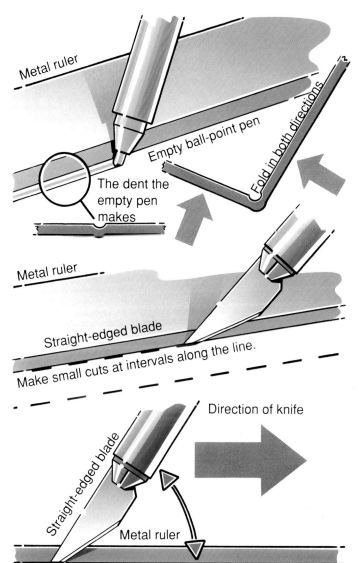

Metal ruler
Empty ball-point pen
The dent the empty pen makes
Fold in both directions

Metal ruler
Straight-edged blade
Make small cuts at intervals along the line.

Direction of knife
Straight-edged blade
Metal ruler
Keep the blade at a constant angle and pull towards you.

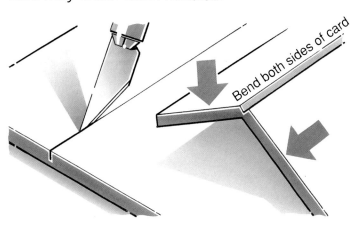

Bend both sides of card

DESIGN TIP

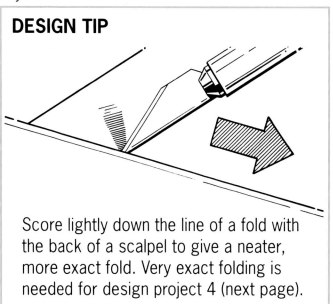

Score lightly down the line of a fold with the back of a scalpel to give a neater, more exact fold. Very exact folding is needed for design project 4 (next page).

A DOCUMENT FOLDER

These pages show you how to make paper and card objects that use very little glue. These objects are made mostly by creasing, folding and tucking.

Fold along the dotted lines.

Cut 3mm away from the fold to allow the card to fold easily down the centre.

Fold

Fold

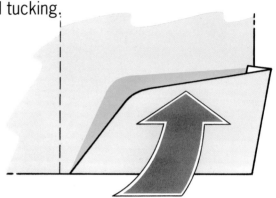

Fold the card upwards and glue the flap behind the folder to create the pocket. The finished product can be decorated in any way.

This is a simple folder made from only one piece of card. The design includes a pocket that has to be glued in one place to make it secure. Decide on the size you want your folder and draw the plan (left) on to it. Add an extra 5mm all the way around the outline so that the folder can close when it is full of papers.

A SIMPLE ENVELOPE

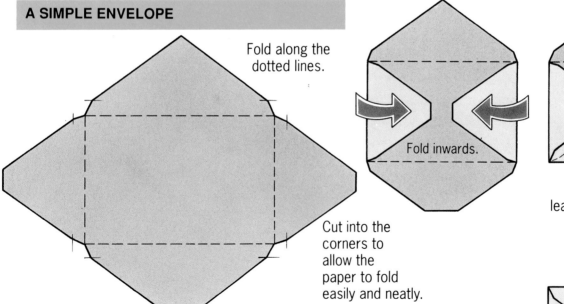

Fold along the dotted lines.

Fold inwards.

Cut into the corners to allow the paper to fold easily and neatly.

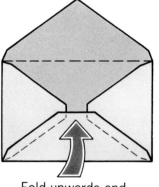

Fold upwards and leave the top flap open.

This is how to make a simple envelope from one sheet of paper. Draw this plan on to your paper to the size you want. To make an envelope for a particular card make sure that the square or rectangle in the middle is the right shape and larger on all sides (by about 3mm).

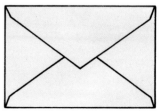

The finished product.

A TUCK-IN LID CARTON

You can use this carton to store pencils, rulers and small pieces of equipment. The carton is made from one piece of card, has to be glued in one place and can be made to any size.

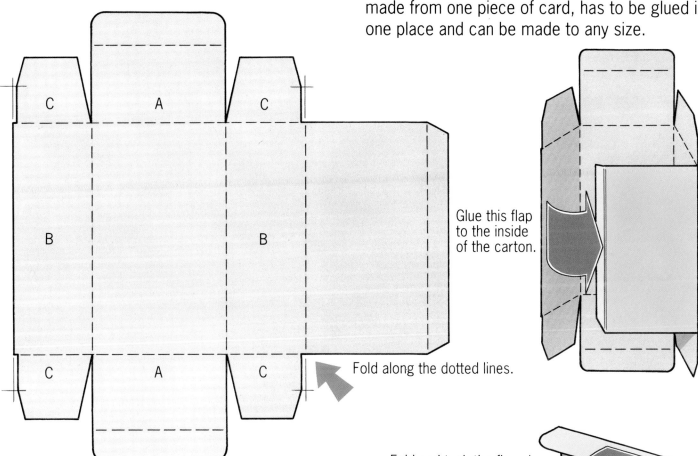

C   A   C

B   B

C   A   C

Fold along the dotted lines.

Glue this flap to the inside of the carton.

Fold and tuck the flaps in to make the carton.

1 Draw up a plan of the carton to the size that you want.

2 Make sure that you draw the plan on to the card so that the grain lies from the top to the bottom of the carton. This will make the card easier to fold.

3 The panels marked A should be 0.5mm shorter than the measurement across the panels marked B so that they tuck in easily.

4 The panels marked B should be exactly the same.

5 The corners marked C should be cut in 1 mm shorter than the length of the card so that the lid and base tuck in easily.

DESIGN PROJECT 4: MAKE A POP-UP CARD

THE BRIEF
The brief is to produce a pop-up card which can be used for any purpose. Copy the card we show you here and then adapt it to your own designs. The card can be made to different sizes because the basic plan we show you here can be repeated as large as you wish.

MATERIALS AND STRUCTURE

You need to use a heavyweight paper as you have to make precise cuts through it without it tearing or breaking. The finished object must also be able to stand up. A smooth cartridge or good quality art paper is usually suitable. Always think about the purpose of the thing you are making and choose a type of paper or card that is strong enough to last and easy to work with.

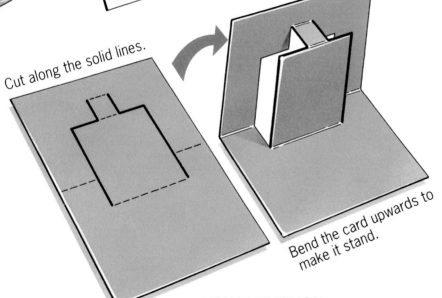

Cut along the solid lines.

Bend the card upwards to make it stand.

IMAGES

The images must not be too fiddly. They must be strong enough to withstand folding in and out frequently and to support themselves.

LEAVE ENOUGH PAPER

The pop-up shapes are cut from the paper itself. You need to save the two end sections of the paper to cover the holes made by cutting out the pop-up.

You should divide up your paper into four equal sections.

The area where you will draw your design.

Fold along the dotted lines.

COPY OUR CARD

The card shown here is made from one sheet of paper. It is a simple design and is half A4 size, so you can make two cards for every A4 sheet you use. The design can be traced and copied. You can hand produce each card, colour it individually and adapt this method to produce cards for any occasion to your own designs.

Cut along the red lines shown. Carefully fold the paper along the dotted lines. Leave a box space for any messages you want to write.

FINISHING OFF

Fold the paper along the dotted lines. Fold the top and the bottom piece of paper behind the pop-up design and glue around the edges. Be careful when you stick down the top and bottom flaps that you do not get any glue on your design, or the card will not open.

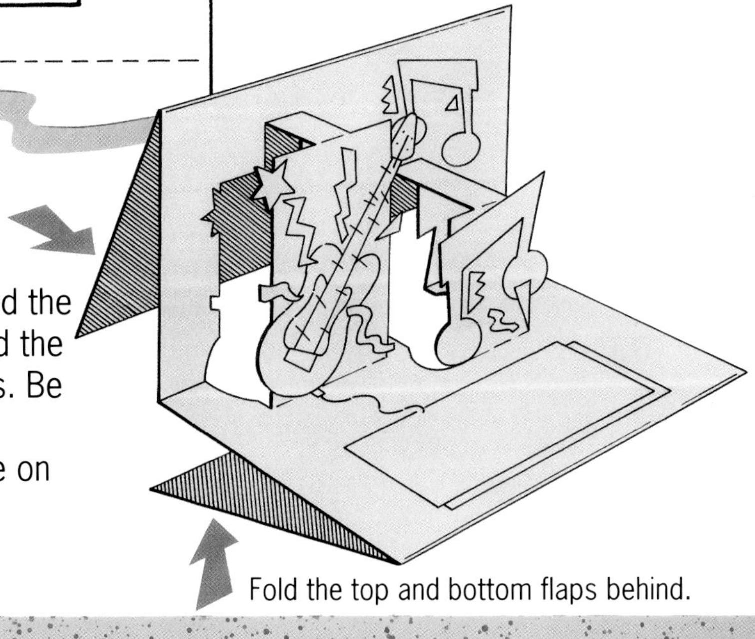

Fold the top and bottom flaps behind.

Now that you have a master design you can adapt the card to anything you want.

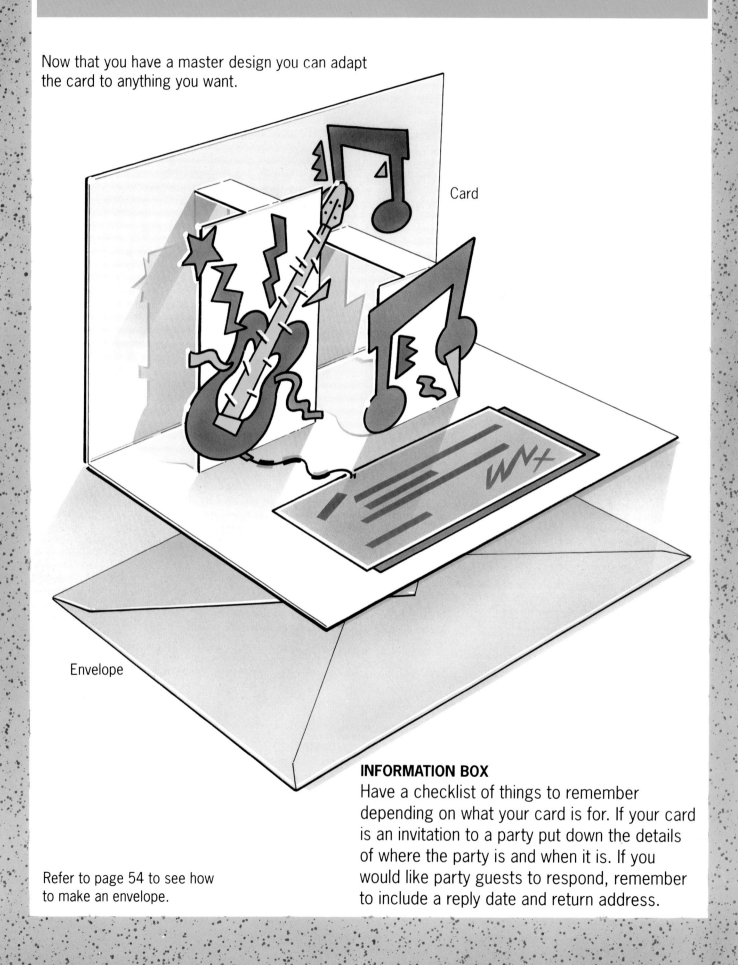

Card

Envelope

Refer to page 54 to see how to make an envelope.

INFORMATION BOX
Have a checklist of things to remember depending on what your card is for. If your card is an invitation to a party put down the details of where the party is and when it is. If you would like party guests to respond, remember to include a reply date and return address.

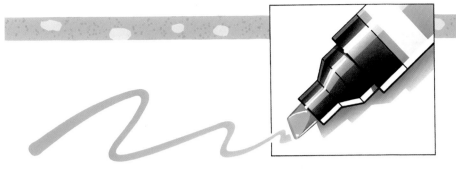

Glossary

acrylic: acrylic paints were originally made from man-made materials in the 1950s in America for covering the outside of wooden houses. From this time onwards acrylics have been used by artists. Acrylic paints can be made to imitate many other kinds of paint such as water-colours and oils depending on how much of any substance, such as water is mixed with them.

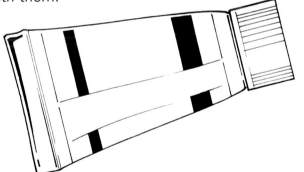

aerosol propellant: air that has been pressurized into a can acts as a force to push the paint through the airbrush out on to the page when the air is released.

air supply line: the tubing that connects the **aerosol propellant** to the airbrush.

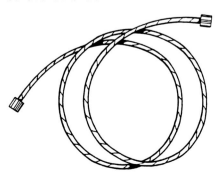
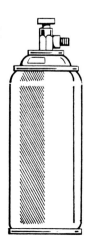

assignment: another name for a brief (see page 23).

atomizes: when paint is momentarily transformed from a liquid to a spray by the **aerosol propellant** of an airbrush.

bevelled: when something, for example a ruler, is bevelled it means that one of its sides is cut away at an angle of 45°. This makes it easier to use.

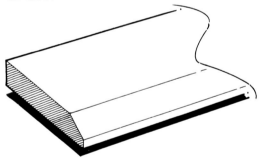

burnisher: this looks a little like a screwdriver or pencil with a flattened metal end. It is used for rubbing dry transfer lettering through on to paper or card.

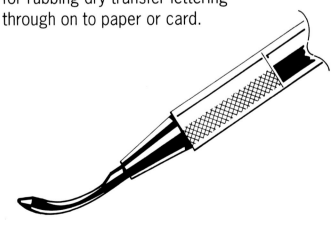

client: the name given to the person or group of people who employ a graphic designer to do a specific job.

colour washes: a paint that has been made thinner by mixing it with a suitable substance, such as water, can be used as a colour wash. The diluted colour is applied with a big brush over the surface of the paper to give the paper a different texture and colour.

drawing board: the name given to the desk that a designer or illustrator uses. A drawing board is different to a normal desk because the desk's surface tilts so that it is easier to draw on.

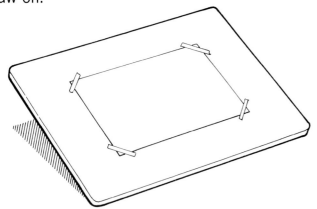

emery board: a small, flat board covered with emery. Emery is a very hard mineral that is ground to a powder and used for polishing. Emery boards are commonly used for polishing fingernails and can also be used to sharpen pencil leads.

emery paper: a piece of paper or cloth covered with emery and used for polishing or sharpening.

gouache: a paint that is like water-colour but has much denser colours. Gouache is very popular with designers and illustrators because it can be used quickly, with very little preparation, produces large, flat areas of colour and looks excellent on paper (as opposed to canvas).

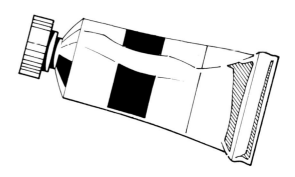

graduated lines: using varying numbers of lines, in varying thicknesses to create a gradual effect.

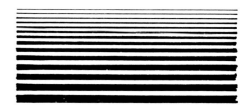

Indian ink: the name of a type of ink that originally came from India and China. Indian ink used to come in the form of a block of solid ink mixed up with glue, but nowadays it can be bought in liquid form. Indian ink is pure black.

logo: originally, this was the name given to a picture that was used instead of a word. Today, when we refer to a logo we mean a symbol or picture that represents a person, a product or a company. This is a logo for a graphic designer.

marketing: people who are employed to sell products to consumers.

media: the term that describes the different types of materials that can be used to draw and paint such as oil paints, water-colours and pastels.

naturalistic: a style of drawing, painting and sculpting that trys to imitate the real world.

non-porous: when something is not porous it means that it will not soak up water.

origami: the Japanese art of folding paper to make beautiful natural forms such as plants and animals.

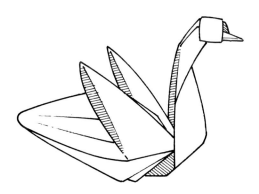

paint reservoir: a compartment in an airbrush where the paint is stored.

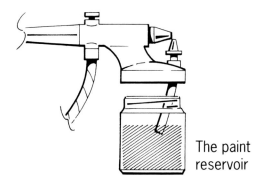

The paint reservoir

quill: a pen made out of a feather. The hollow part of the feather is cut lengthways once with a fine knife. This cut allows ink to flow through the hollow so the feather can be used as a pen.

realize: to take an idea and work it out visually into an end product.

sable: the name of a type of hair taken from the tail of a sable marten, a mink-like animal. These hairs are used to make the finest paint brushes because they are soft, strong and form a very fine point so that details can be painted easily.

spring bow (compass): a compass that has a screw-thread locking device between its two arms to hold it in position when drawing a circle.

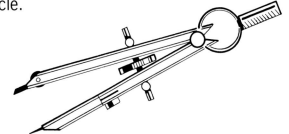

water-soluable: a liquid or solid that can be diluted with water.

Useful Information and Addresses

BASIC SUPPLIES
All the items metioned in this book can be bought in graphic supply shops or office and stationary supply stores such as WH Smith and Rymans.

PRINTS AND COPIES
You can get prints and photocopies made of your work at print-copy shops such as Kall Kwik and Prontaprint.

FINDING THE RIGHT SUPPLIER
To locate your nearest specialist graphic store contact;

DELTA, the Graphic and Reprographic Suppliers Association, 25/27 Oxford Street, London W1R 1RF
Tel: 071 734 2971
Fax: 071 494 1764

THE DESIGN MUSEUM
Always remember to look around you for old and new examples of design. Many museums, such the Victoria and Albert in London, have twentieth century galleries that are dedicated to the best designs of this century. There is also a museum dedicated entirely to design in London. The Design Museum at Bulters Wharf SE1 (the nearest tube station is Tower Hill on the District line) is open seven days a week.

FURTHER READING
You will find that many graphics shops have a selection of specialist design books. If you do not want to buy any books then remember to search out the crafts section in your local library for books to borrow.

Index

A **bold** number shows the entry is illustrated on that page.